THE
IDIOT'S
GUIDE TO

Being an Expectant Father

by Joe Kelly

ALPHA

A member of Penguin Group (USA) Inc.

For my wonderful children, Nia Kelly and Mavis Gruver.

ALPHA BOOKS

Published by the Penguin Group

Penguin Group (USA) Inc., 375 Hudson Street, New York, New York 10014, USA

Penguin Group (Canada), 90 Eglinton Avenue East, Suite 700, Toronto, Ontario M4P 2Y3, Canada (a division of Pearson Penguin Canada Inc.)

Penguin Books Ltd., 80 Strand, London WC2R 0RL, England

Penguin Ireland, 25 St. Stephen's Green, Dublin 2, Ireland (a division of Penguin Books Ltd.)

Penguin Group (Australia), 250 Camberwell Road, Camberwell, Victoria 3124, Australia (a division of Pearson Australia Group Pty. Ltd.)

Penguin Books India Pvt. Ltd., 11 Community Centre, Panchsheel Park, New Delhi—110 017, India

Penguin Group (NZ), 67 Apollo Drive, Rosedale, North Shore, Auckland 1311, New Zealand (a division of Pearson New Zealand Ltd.)

Penguin Books (South Africa) (Pty.) Ltd., 24 Sturdee Avenue, Rosebank, Johannesburg 2196, South Africa

Penguin Books Ltd., Registered Offices: 80 Strand, London WC2R 0RL, England

Contents

Introduction

To all future fathers expecting their first, you will
not have all of the answers, and yes, you will wonder how you are going to afford the formula and
diapers, but it is the greatest experience known to
man.

Pregnant Pauses

I was in the birthing room and that is an
experience you do not want to miss
(although I could have done without the
bone crunching grip my wife gave my
hand).
—Ron

So you're a dad-to-be. There's a new baby entering
your life. Congratulations!!!

Now, take a deep breath. And another one. Then,
disengage the panic button for just a moment,
while I tell you that you can do this Daddy thing.

For thousands of years (or millions, depending who
you believe), men have become fathers. The overwhelming majority did it without ever reading a
book. That long historic and genetic heritage lays a
pretty solid foundation for you.

What this book does is help guide you through the
first few months as a father—a job that starts well
before the object of your fathering (the baby)
comes out of hiding in the womb.

It's important to know that, despite those millennia of experience, it takes conscious effort (and sometimes even a bit of pushiness) for a man to stay involved in pregnancy, birth, and child-rearing nowadays.

The challenge is a lot like the one a guy faces in a modern-day wedding. Before a wedding, there's a storm of activity and decisions underway—often just out of the groom's sight or reach. Relatives and family friends (some you've never met or even heard of) suddenly seem to have veto power over a day that's supposed to belong to you and your bride.

Relatives and family friends can do the same thing during pregnancy, elbowing the expectant dad out of the way so they can reach the expectant mom with unsolicited advice, "let me tell you about my labor" horror stories, and ironclad suggestions for what to name the baby.

To top it off, you and your partner probably never got pregnant or decided to adopt before. And it's not likely that Dad or Granddad set you on his knee to regale you with tales of when Mom was pregnant with you.

You can take comfort in this, though: You're not alone. Most men lack a surefire road map for making the Clark Kent–like transformation from regular guy to something bigger than Superman—*father*.

But you have this book, don't you? So stick this travel guide in your back pocket, sports coat, toolbox, or glove compartment—so you can pull it out whenever you need to.

This book will show you:

- Why and how to avoid being left behind in the roller coaster of doctors visits, birthing classes, butt-in-ski relatives, labor and delivery, and the first days and weeks of your child's new life.

- How to use your provider and protector instincts to help ensure a healthy, enjoyable pregnancy for you, your partner, and your baby (or babies).

- How to share this miracle with your partner (and your baby) as fully as possible.

When you're done with *The Pocket Idiot's Guide to Being an Expectant Father*, you won't have a magic cape or x-ray powers to see you through to perfect fatherhood. (That's because there's no such thing as magic capes, x-ray vision, or perfect fathering.) But you will have a beginner's toolbox for the most exciting job you'll ever have, and you'll know how to keep your toolbox well stocked.

Welcome to the brotherhood of Dads!

Just a couple notes:

1. Having a pregnant partner isn't the only way to be an expectant father. If you, or you and your partner are adopting a child, then you're expectant, too. There are a lot of parallels between going through the arduous, often confusing adoption process and going through ... well, pregnancy! So this book works for the adopting dad, too. As

   you read, substitute "adoption process" for
   "pregnancy" and you'll get the idea.

2. Sometimes I think the term "partner" perfectly describes the rich, complicated, shared,
   spiritual nature of the 25+ years I've spent
   (so far) loving my wife. Other times, it sounds
   like a cold description someone in a shady
   law firm. But, we'll use "partner" in the book
   anyway, because "wife" doesn't apply to some
   folks, and for others (like adopting couples),
   it may not even be a significant other of the
   opposite sex who is pregnant. Bottom line:
   "Partner" is an imperfect word. But as good
   partners, we'll shake on it and move on.

3. Some babies are boys and some are girls
   (This really is a *Complete Idiot's Guide!*). So
   I'll sometimes call the baby she, and other
   times, he. I'll try to avoid "it" altogether.

Extras

Look for these handy sidebars throughout the book—
they have the important concepts you'll need to get
the most out of an event that will already be the
time of your life.

Crib Notes

> Key concepts and facts you'll need to
> remember, and important questions to ask
> (yourself and others) during the pregnancy.

Dads and Dollars _____

Financial pointers, because these babies cost big bucks! (Which is cheap, because they're priceless.)

OB/GYN _____

OB/GYN also stands for "Oh Brother, Grab Your Notebook." Hints for navigating the mysterious ways of the medical world. "Yes, Virginia, men do go to the gynecologist."

Pregnant Pauses _____

Things to ponder as you begin the most amazing thing you've ever done.

Acknowledgments

Thanks to Armin Brott for writing the Bible of Expectant Fathering, Dr. Joy Dorscher, M.D., and Judge David Peterson for their expert guidance, and to the men of the national nonprofit Dads and Daughters for sharing their stories. Thanks to Coleen O'Shea, Steve Knauss, Mike Sanders, Ginny Munroe, and Billy Fields for helping me birth the book. Most of all, thanks to my wife Nancy Gruver and my children, Mavis and Nia, who made me an expectant father all those years ago.

Trademarks

All terms mentioned in this book that are known to be or are suspected of being trademarks or service marks have been appropriately capitalized. Alpha Books and Penguin Group (USA) Inc. cannot attest to the accuracy of this information. Use of a term in this book should not be regarded as affecting the validity of any trademark or service mark.

Where's the Owner's Manual?

In This Chapter

- There is no owner's manual
- People say the darndest things
- Sharing the news
- Am I nuts?

You've heard that you're expecting. If your first reaction is panic, it's not a big deal. Really! Almost every father freezes when thinking about the enormous responsibility of being a dad. (In fact, fatherly panic attacks may happen regularly over the next 18, 21, ..., or 50 years, so get used to them.)

You and I grew up learning that a father's biggest responsibilities are to provide and protect. As soon as you know that you're expecting, you'll feel a lot more protective of your partner, both physically and psychologically. You'll also start to wonder whether you can be a good enough provider.

Here's how one veteran father puts it:

> The only thing I really remember clearly when my wife announced she was pregnant, was being scared as hell. Did I make enough money to afford a family? Would I know what I was doing when trying to raise a child? Would I be able to share my wife with another person without getting upset and angry at the amount of time she would have to spend with the baby?
>
> I found out that if you wait until you can afford a child you will never have one, and that I had no idea what I was doing. After the baby was home, my last question became moot; in fact I was a little jealous that my wife got to spend more time with the baby than I did!

 Crib Notes

You are never fully prepared for the birth of your child, even if this is not your first time around. That's because this baby has never been born before. So don't fight it, accept it!

You don't need a lot of money to be a good provider. Your baby needs your money, but she needs your time and attention even more—at least until she's a teenager (when she'll *think* she needs just the money, but she'll be wrong).

The good news is that your protector and provider instincts will be very handy for the next nine months, and the next couple of decades (yup, most kids stick around at least that long). Using those instincts wisely (and not overusing them), you can do more than anyone else to make this pregnancy the healthiest and most enjoyable one possible for you, your partner, and your new child.

Plus, along with the panic, you'll also start feeling great pride in your accomplishment. Rightly so! And pride will continue to be a great comfort and motivation through all your days as a father.

There Is No Owner's Manual

When you hear that you're going to have a baby, you may feel a deep, intense need to find the perfect owner's manual for having and raising him. That's good! It is nature's way of telling you how important you are to raising your soon-to-be baby. And after all, we're guys, so we like to have the instruction manual handy (even if our partners insist that we never, ever read one).

However, there is a little glitch. There is no owner's manual. There isn't even an AAA road map. There is no set-in-stone formula for the pregnancy, your child, his life from infancy to adulthood, or your life from his infancy to adulthood.

Nor is there any controlling legal authority to tell you how to do your fathering. I like the line from the movie *Parenthood* when Keanu Reeves's character

Tod says, "You need a license to buy a dog or drive a car. Hell, you even need a license to catch a fish. But they'll let any [expletive deleted] a**hole be a father."

The Tricks of the Trade

If you're reading this book, you clearly don't want to be an [expletive deleted] a**hole father. That's very good news for you, your partner, and your kid(s). So how do you get the information and guidance you wish you could find in that nonexistent, good-for-all-makes-and-models owner's manual? This book is a good start.

Here are several other excellent sources of guidance, in order of importance:

1. **Your gut.** Nature has given us the means to conceive, birth, and rear children for millennia. There's plenty of good animal instinct in our history and our genes. So don't be afraid to trust your gut. After all, there'd be no new child without your seminal participation, so you're pretty tightly connected to her.

2. **Your partner.** You're in this together, so share the experience and communicate, communicate, communicate. And remember that our tools of communication include twice as many ears as mouths (in other words, listen more than you talk). Did I mention that it's important to communicate?

3. **Your family.** They can be a great source of what to do in successful parenting ... or what not to do. Or usually, both. Take what you need from your family history and leave the rest.

4. **Other fathers and mothers.** Yes, other parents are willing—even eager—to share their wisdom. Who doesn't like being used as an expert? So talk (and listen) to them, especially the dads.

Crib Notes

Nature provides just about every man with the ability to raise a child. It's been that way since time began. It pays to listen to your natural, nurturing instincts—you've got 'em, so use 'em!

We'll give a lot of attention later on to learning from and communicating with your partner and your gut. For just a moment, let's look at the other people on the list.

Can Your Parents Be Salvaged?

For some of us, our parents and stepparents seem a mother lode (why aren't there father lodes?) of good ways to parent. For some of us, our parents seem more like a junk heap of bad examples to be plowed under as soon as possible.

For most of us, though, our parents have both gold and dross.

Your next few months as an expectant father are a great time to take an honest, detached look at how your parents, stepparents, grandparents, and others parented you and your siblings. Even if that view shows only a tall pile of junk, there is still probably something in that pile to salvage. As my grandmother used to say, "Even a stopped clock is right twice a day." (Of course, that was back before digital clocks, but you get the idea.)

Pregnant Pauses

Write down five good things your father, stepfather, or grandfather did that you want to be sure you do for your child.

Write down five things your father, stepfather, or grandfather did that you want to be sure you avoid doing to your child.

Save these lists, and pull them out again on your child's first birthday.

Remember that the same parental behavior can feel great or terrible, depending on the circumstances. Your dad's hugs may have been the most comforting thing in the world some days, and felt smothering on others. One day, his encouragement to excel made you feel proud under the spotlight of his attention. Another day, it felt like rejection of who you are. Being a father is a complicated thing. So is being a child.

Becoming a father will probably change the way you feel about your stepparents and parents. You may feel more forgiving and appreciative of them, or maybe less. Either way, there's a lot you can learn from them.

The key is taking a detached look at how they parented. Now is a great time to do this, because you are not yet swept away by the distractions and intense emotions of parenting your own crying, giggling, walking, sassing, and adorable child. Still, an expectant father is still a father, and you see things in a different light now—including how you were raised.

Do I Really Want Some Other Parents' Advice?

Remember those millennia worth of fathers that came before you? Quite a few of them are still alive and kicking. Don't let them go to waste.

Let's suppose my four nearest neighbors and I added up the ages of all our respective children. The total would surpass 250. When we five guys get together, there are more than two and a half centuries of fathering experience in the room. One of these guys has been married twice, one has a son with disabilities, one has twins, two have grandchildren. It is tough to come up with a situation one of us hasn't encountered.

It would be kind of silly not to take advantage of all that experience and wisdom. Despite this, however, we seldom talk to each other about being dads. We're more comfortable discussing intricacies of the office football pool than the pros and cons of teaching an infant to swim.

Fortunately, you don't have to repeat those "strong and silent" or "parenting is for sissies" patterns. (Parenting is most definitely not for sissies, whatever they are.) So build up your courage to ask an experienced father for advice. Or just ask him to tell stories about when he and his partner were adopting or pregnant. The odds that he'll be flattered and happy to chat are much better than the odds of winning that football pool.

And don't forget those veteran moms. Girls grow up hearing as much about parenting as we heard about baseball. So when they grow up and become moms, they can also be valuable coaches for us rookies.

People Say the Darndest Things

Families and friends can be peculiar about a lot of things. That includes pregnancy and adoption. So don't be surprised if family or friends (yours and hers both) say or do some goofy or even inconsiderate things when they hear your good news. This next section will prepare you for just about any reaction to your new status as expectant dad.

What Your Partner Needs You to Say

Remember that old Paul Anka hit, "Having My Baby"? Here's a tip: Don't ever say, "*She's* having *my* baby." (Sorry, Paul!)

Instead, say, "*We're* having *our* baby." Seem like a minor point? Well, it's not. When you say "She's having my baby," it sounds like you own both the baby and the mom (you don't)—a sentiment that may very well make your partner want to scream.

The whole process of being an expectant father and a new dad is a "we" thing. You and your partner made this baby together, or decided together to adopt this baby. When you stop to think about it, that's really a miracle! So you both should do all you can to make sure you share it all.

Start by always remembering to tell people "We're having a baby," "We're expecting," "We're adopting," or "We're pregnant." Then, insist that others use similar terminology when referring to your pregnancy. That will help everyone (including you) get used to the idea that *you are a full partner* in this making and raising a baby gig.

Using this sort of verbiage also helps you avoid being shunted aside (or skulking away) when it comes to decisions about the pregnancy and arrival of the new child.

The other thing you should be sure to say to your partner is "You're beautiful" and "I love you." Often.

Most days, these words will come quite easily. Many expectant fathers (myself included) report that their partners seemed to glow during pregnancy. And having a baby might well be the most intimate thing two people can do together.

Other days, when hormones and energy (yours and hers both) are riding the tilt-a-whirl, it may take every ounce of discipline you have to tell her that she's beautiful and lovable. Do it anyway.

You see, nature has a way of making mothers (and, sometimes, fathers) forget the pain of labor and the uproar of pregnancy, probably so that women will get back on the tilt-a-whirl, have more babies, and keep the human race going.

But women always seem to remember when their partners say something mean or ill-tempered, even if it's in the midst of pregnancy, when irrational hormones rule. More important, though, is your partner's need for reassurance that you still find her captivating. Believe me, your partner may be at her most captivating in the days after the baby arrives, and it's a wonderful thing for a daddy to see.

Telling the Good News

Some pregnant and adopting parents want to tell everyone, right away, that they are expecting. Some delay their news until all danger of miscarriage or adoption-derailment-by-red-tape has passed. Some want certain friends or relatives to know the news months before other ones, and so swear the former to secrecy. Others wait until people ask them before sharing the news.

Any of these choices can work fine. The most important thing is for *both* partners to have the *same* approach.

It's no fun when Aunt Suzy effusively congratulates your partner after your partner had already decided to wait another month before dealing with Aunt Suzy. It really sucks when *you're* the one who spilled the beans.

Dads and Dollars

As soon as you and your partner are pregnant, tell your insurance company. Call to find out how to "officially" let them know that a baby is on the way. They might require a letter, a filled-out form, or the phone call alone might be enough. But don't wait—the sooner your insurer knows you're expecting, the less hassle you'll encounter when all the birth-related bills roll in.

If your income is low, start looking into your eligibility for Medicaid and other publicly subsidized insurance—your county Social Services Department can get you started.

If you're uninsured, be sure to shop around for hospitals and OB/GYN "package" arrangements, where the hospital and doctor agree to perform certain set services for a single fee. But keep in mind, these arrangements seldom cover "unusual" circumstances, like the baby having to stay extra days in the hospital.

The question of who, when, and in what order to tell your good news will probably be the first major communication challenge the two of you face as parents. How you handle this question may influence how your parenting team handles future challenges. If you learn from your mistakes, and improve your communication and flexibility, that's great. If you cement a pattern of judging your results by which one of you "wins" an argument, that's going to take the fun (and proficiency) out of raising your child.

So use the "who do we tell when?" challenge as a dry run. It can teach you a lot about how to work well together as parents once your kid shows up—because he raises the stakes a lot higher than Aunt Suzy ever will.

> **Crib Notes** _____
>
> If you and your partner have gone through a miscarriage in the past, you're likely to feel vulnerable, especially in the early stages of another pregnancy. Give yourself every permission to put your needs first when deciding who to tell and when.

If You're Not Married

If you're not married when you and your partner are expecting, you will surely run into people (including relatives) who are less than pleased that you're having a baby. For example, people who think marriage should always come before pregnancy (and intercourse), or people who think it is wrong for homosexual couples or single people to adopt.

Over the long term, the legal status of your relationship with your partner and the child is far more important than what your grandmother thinks now. We'll cover the legal stuff in Chapter 6, but sharing the news with disapproving relatives, friends, colleagues, and acquaintances is challenging.

Be open, honest, accepting, and roll with the punches. My partner and I weren't married when we got pregnant (although we did marry before our twins were born), so my grandfather expressed serious disappointment at the news. I always craved his approval, so it hurt when he told me how he felt. But, being the wise man he was, he didn't belabor the point (since he knew belaboring it wouldn't keep us from having a baby) and he didn't stop showing his love. He was as happy as anyone when our babies were born, and having a happy great-grandfather was far more important for my kids than whether my feelings were bruised for a few days by his disappointment.

Pregnant Pauses

In a sense, get selfish. Tell, don't ask, your family what they will be doing for you when the kids are born. If you've got family close, so much the better, but even if you don't you should start setting up your help network now! Arrange for people to bring hot meals the first two weeks, find someone you trust to baby-sit occasionally, and introduce yourself to everyone in your neighborhood who has children under two years old.

—Bob

Sure, a relative's reaction may hurt for a short time. But if everyone acts like an adult, then the hurt will soon be forgotten in the excitement of your beautiful baby.

If some people choose not to act like adults, well, there's nothing you can do to change them, so don't try. You're far better off putting that energy into raising your kid well, so that when she becomes an adult, *she'll* act like one.

If You're Adopting

According to the National Adoption Information Clearinghouse (naic.acf.hhs.gov/), adoption is "the permanent legal transfer of parenting rights and responsibilities from one family to another." More than 125,000 children are adopted in the United States each year, and the number of foreign-born children adopted by U.S. families has nearly tripled in the past decade.

Of course, adoption is a lot more complicated than dry definitions and statistics.

Unfortunately, not everyone realizes this. When you tell family and friends that you're adopting, you may encounter uninformed questions (like "How will my 'real' children feel?"), or even blatantly bigoted attitudes (especially if adopting from overseas). You need a plan that:

- Addresses misconceptions and prejudiced comments directly.
- Takes advantage of every opportunity to teach others about adoption.

- Shows patience with people who may not know as much as you do about adoption.
- Allows you to decide how much information you're willing to share.
- Is sensitive to the mixed feelings some relatives may have.

It's important to develop, use, and modify this plan now because you will need it when you meet new people throughout your baby's childhood. Plus, in those later years, your child will probably be listening in when you respond to these inevitable questions.

Be aware that some relatives may not immediately jump for joy at your news. As Patricia Irwin Johnston says in *Launching a Baby's Adoption* (Perspectives Press, 1998), your parents may have to get over (and even grieve) feelings that their genetic heritage won't be passed on, or thoughts that this won't be a "real" grandchild.

Don't worry too much, because parents and other relatives usually get over these feelings pretty quickly. So don't take their feelings personally, and be patient. Your sensitivity will help hasten the time when Grandma is excited about the idea of your child, regardless of what womb he came from.

Make sure you are clear and comfortable with your feelings about welcoming your child into your family. Your clarity will make it easier for relatives and friends, and give you a better foundation for confronting any challenges that arise now, or later.

Dealing with Unwelcome (and Downright Rude) Reactions

People say some amazing things to expectant fathers and mothers. They also say some amazingly dumb things. Here's just a few:

- Are you sure you're the father?
- I didn't put on that much weight when I was pregnant.
- She's pregnant? Now, maybe you will finally get a decent job.
- My sister hadn't felt a kick yet either, and her baby has Down syndrome.

This is the time for you to put on your "father as protector" gear. If your partner or you get upset when the next door neighbor starts sharing awful stories from her 36-hour delivery or 36-month adoption process, politely and firmly tell the neighbor to stop.

Listen to a veteran dad:

> When we told a good friend that we were pregnant, she immediately told us her horror stories, and then started telling stories from her relatives and even people she'd met on airplanes. I just had to say enough. I said, "We need to change the subject now." Later on in our pregnancy, some of her experiences did help us. It's just that she was more sensitive in how she approached it, and we knew more about what information and support we needed.

If someone is just plain rude and obnoxious, don't be afraid to promptly don your shining armor, take your partner, and walk away.

On the other hand, most people say wonderful, supportive things to expectant parents. So be sure to stick around, take off your armor, and bask in those comments!

Am I Nuts?

You get extra points for knowing the answer to this question.

(*Hint:* The answer is no.)

Sometimes you may feel a bit nuts, but you can be pretty sure that all of your reactions are normal and that most other expectant fathers have felt, done, and thought the same things.

Nature Calls

You may think that nature, hormones, and animal instincts have taken over your partner during pregnancy, transforming her (at least sometimes) into a barely recognizable creature.

You're right. But did you know that the same may be true for you, too? In his wonderful book, *The Expectant Father: Facts, Tips and Advice for Dads-to-Be* (Abbeville Press, 2002), Armin Brott reports on research showing that an expectant father's levels of the hormones prolactin and cortisol increase during his partner's pregnancy. They don't go up as much as the mother's levels do, but they still rise.

That may be one explanation for why so many of us experience "sympathy pains" during pregnancy.

It's very common for expectant fathers to have a kind of morning sickness, sleep more, feel stomach cramps, crave unusual foods, engage in "nesting" behavior, and have unpredictable mood swings—all things that are usually seen as exclusive to expectant moms.

Unfortunately, when these things happen to an expectant dad, they are often ridiculed—even by the mom, who may figure (perhaps correctly) that her symptoms are more intense than yours. But that doesn't mean your symptoms are imaginary.

This is one more time to remember the importance of communication between you and your partner. Patience and listening are key steps, along with remembering that good communication doesn't flourish in an environment of continual scorekeeping about which person is getting the raw or well done end of the stick. Who eats barbecued sticks, anyway?

Many people will dismiss your "sympathetic pains" as merely psychological. To which one can only reply that any parent who dismisses psychology will be flying so blind that he'll crash land into one mountain after another.

Psychology and hormones are both quite real, and expectant fathers' "sympathy pains" are acknowledged by the medical community as *couvade syndrome* (*couvade* is French for "to hatch").

Brott writes, "Various studies estimate that as many as 90 percent of American fathers experience couvade syndrome." That's no surprise when you remember that nature has known for eons that pregnancy happens to two people, not just one.

The emotional and physical feelings you have during pregnancy or adoption may not seem normal. They aren't, because you're not normally pregnant or adopting. But those sensations *are* natural, real, and ultimately useful.

In fact, nature provides them for very good reasons— to help you empathize with your partner, to prepare you for the labor and birth, and to trigger your instincts to nurture, protect, and provide.

Need we say more?

Fear: Can I Provide and Protect?

If you're reading this book, odds are nearly 100 percent that the answer is yes. But you may have to rethink your definitions, too.

Past generations of dads had a pretty narrow definition of being a provider: Provider equals paycheck. Fortunately, that's changing for the current generation of fathers. One recent study indicates that fathers under 40 are more willing than those over 40 to forgo a raise or promotion at work if it means they get more time at home with their kids.

Right now, your partner needs you to provide her with affection, physical and emotional support, and help in protecting her (and the baby) from people, places, and things that threaten their well-being.

So make sure you have (and keep) a broad and healthy definition of being a provider. Yes, you have to contribute financially (duh!), but your partner (and, pretty soon, your child) will also need you to provide a large allowance of your time and attention. Give both child and mother a full and steady dose of your energy, affection, masculinity, stories, physicality, love of risk, heritage—all the wonderful things that make up a man and father.

My daughters are adults now, and I couldn't tell you my weekly pay the year they were born. But I can tell you in great detail about the first time I heard them laugh, or the colic-filled night that I got them to sleep when my wife couldn't. You can't buy memories like these. In other words, full engagement in your child's life is way more important than a full wallet.

So when you panic about whether you can afford to have this baby, and whether you can provide for her, remember this: Any man, rich or poor, can provide *himself* to his children. In fact, the everyday activities of nurturing your child (the "exciting" experiences like diaper changing) do more to build your relationship than any bank account does.

Dads and Dollars

Providing is far more than a paycheck. No matter how much or how little money you have, the most valuable thing you must provide your child (and your partner) is you.

Do Fathers Matter?

Too often, we fathers see ourselves as secondary parents. Too often, our culture sees us as second-class parents. Both viewpoints are wrong.

Dads aren't more important than moms, nor are they less important. Dads and moms are different; when it comes to kids or parents, *viva la difference!*

As a father, you have immense influence on each and every one of your children and/or stepchildren. Some fathers don't seem to realize that they have this influence. Others don't seem to want it. But that doesn't change the fact that every one of us fathers *has* it. So we may as well use it as positively as possible.

You've already started to do that by becoming an involved and intentional partner in this pregnancy. So now is a good time to examine the difference between having influence and having control.

Pregnant Pauses

Fathering requires faith. You have to trust that your influence and involvement makes a difference. Even if you can't always see the results of your fathering, your child needs you to keep being her dad.

You can influence this pregnancy, but you can't predict exactly how it will go. You will influence your kids, but ultimately you can't control them or guarantee any outcomes for them. This may seem obvious, but it's not always easy to remember in the heat of fathering.

We can never know with absolute certainty what will happen to our kids, or how our actions today will affect our child's life in 10 years (if he even remembers them).

To a certain degree, being a father means getting comfortable with uncertainty. From the days of midnight feedings to the days of midnight curfews, fathering also means getting comfortable with a certain level of discomfort.

Ultimately, being a father is about having faith. Faith is the evidence of things unseen, and our children's futures are unseeable. But have faith that your positive involvement in your children's lives makes a difference. And pretty soon, you'll start seeing the evidence of that influence, even though the picture may not be complete or ever finish developing.

Whatever you do as a dad, keep the faith!

The Least You Need to Know

- Trust your gut because Nature provides every man with the basic tools to be a father.
- Your partner needs your support and affection every day.
- Expecting can be great practice and preparation for fathering.

- You can learn things from other parents—even your own.
- People will say off-the-wall things to you, but roll with the punches.
- Odds are that your feelings, thoughts, and actions are all natural, even if they are a bit unusual.

Chapter 2

From Foreplay to Fetus: The Pregnancy Primer

In This Chapter

- What health class left out
- Where sperm come from
- Where eggs come from
- Where babies come from
- Inside the womb month by month

If you paid close attention during health class, this next chapter may be old hat. But if you're like a lot of guys, your health class might have been less than forthcoming about sex. Or like me, you may never even have had health class at all.

To feel confident while you're expecting, and to be the most use to your partner, it's important to know the basics of pregnancy. So call this chapter your pregnancy primer, or "What's going on in there?"

How Pregnancy Begins and Progresses

We begin this chapter with a song by another over-the-hill act. When the day comes to start telling your child the facts of life, remember that ancient Sonny and Cher tune, "It Takes Two, Baby." Strip away all the details, and getting pregnant boils down to two people having intercourse (an activity where stripping down usually helps things along).

The exception, in these modern times, is in vitro fertilization (IVF), surrogate mothering, and other medical options that will pop up in the coming years. Either way, you should know how pregnancy starts and progresses, as well as the layout of the plumbing that gets the baby rolling.

OB/GYN

The most complete and easy-to-understand explanation of our sexual organs is in the book *All About Sex: A Family Resource on Sex and Sexuality* by Planned Parenthood (Three Rivers Press, 1997). A great resource on the details of pregnancy itself is the ubiquitous *What to Expect When You're Expecting* by Heidi Murkoff, Arlene Eisenberg, and Sandee Hathaway (Workman), which is updated every few years.

My descriptions here are very basic. If you think you know all this backward and forward, you can skip ahead (although it probably wouldn't hurt to read this anyway ... I mean, aren't you captivated by my writing yet?).

Male Plumbing

You have reproductive organs while you are still in the womb, and they start out looking exactly like a female's organs. But then the two sexes' organs start to develop uniquely.

The purpose of the male reproductive organs is to produce (or reproduce?) reproductive cells. Logical, no? Those cells are called sperm, and they look like tadpoles—if you're peering through a super strong microscope (or watching one of those grainy health class films).

It all starts in your testes (or testicles), those two small balls in your scrotum (the sac that hangs below your penis). One part of the teste produces androgen, the male sex hormones (including testosterone), which stimulates the other part of the teste to start forming sperm. You start making sperm in puberty and you never stop. We'll bypass speculation about what symbolism (if any) should be attached to that fact, and just say: it's true.

Sperm spend a lot of time in tubes, and take a very round about trip through our bodies before jumping out. The testes have 750 feet of wound-tight tubes, and the sperm leave those and travel into another coiled tube, the epididymis, (there's one above each teste). This is where the sperm grow up and get their tails, and then hang around in storage until ejaculation.

When you get sexually stimulated, tiny muscles start pushing your sperm out of the epididymis and through the vas deferens, one more tube. This tube is more direct (relatively), travels north, then makes a big circle next to your bladder. The vas deferens deposits the sperm into the seminal vesicles, where they pick up seminal fluid to feed the sperm and give them something in which to "spread their tails" and start swimming.

Your sperm then move down into your prostate gland, which secretes a milky fluid into your urethra (hang in there, I'll tell you what a urethra is in a second), so your sperm can really cut loose for a swim. Just below the prostate are the two Cowper's glands, named for William Cowper (1666–1709), the English surgeon who discovered them—in *The English Patient*, no doubt.

Cowper's glands also send a fluid into the urethra to facilitate the sperms' swimming journey. The urethra (drum roll please) is the tube in your penis through which semen (the combination of all this fluid and sperm) passes. It's also the tube through which your urine passes, but never at the same time as your semen, because a series of muscles act as gates to let only one or the other through.

Surrounding the urethra in your penis is tissue called *corpus cavernosa* and *corpus spongiosum*—poetic Latin terms that suggest caverns and sponges.

Basically, these caverns and sponges fill with blood when you get aroused—and that's why your penis gets large (an erection) during sex. The erection later collapses, because the blood leaves and goes back where it came from.

When all systems are working normally, a muscle below your prostate gland will "open the gate" and let the semen into your urethra. The combination of the blood coursing through your penis and other muscle action causes the semen to rush through the urethra and out the opening at the end of your penis. This is called ejaculation.

If you look at a diagram, the whole process doesn't seem very efficient. It starts in your testes, which are millimeters from the tip of your penis. But the sperm travel in a long route (almost a figure-eight) before they gather up all their tools, leave "home," and head off to their appointed work.

Pregnant Pauses

Males don't begin making their reproductive cells (sperm) until they reach puberty, and they continue producing them into old age. A female is born with all the reproductive cells (eggs) that she'll ever have. Eggs begin being released every month at puberty, and stop being released after menopause.

If the end of your penis is inside (or even close to, as health teachers reminded us) the vagina of a fertile female at ejaculation, then pregnancy is possible. As far as the biology of pregnancy goes, the rest is up to your sperm and the plumbing of the female.

Female Plumbing

A female's reproductive organs spend exponentially more time bringing a pregnancy to completion than a male's do—but the female's plumbing is more straightforward. Well, it has a lot fewer tubes, at any rate.

The visible part of your partner's reproductive organs is the vulva, which includes the labia majora and labia minora; they basically cover and protect the vagina, urethra, and clitoris. In a woman, the urethra only carries urine (nothing else) and the clitoris' only purpose (a *very* important one) is to give a female sexual pleasure.

For this discussion, the vagina is top priority. The vagina is a moist, flexible tunnel that starts at the vulva and ends four or more inches inside the body at the cervix. It holds the penis during intercourse, and that's where the sperm go when they leave you.

On the other side of the cervix is the uterus, which is about 3 inches long when a woman isn't pregnant. Obviously, it is also very flexible and gets much bigger when she is pregnant. For a sperm to trigger the start of a pregnancy, it has to pass through the cervix and travel all the way up the uterus to the tiny opening of a fallopian tube.

There are two fallopian tubes on the north end of the uterus, one coming in from the west, the other from the east.

> **Crib Notes**
>
> The versatile vagina also expands to become the birth canal that the baby passes through. *All About Sex* describes the vagina as like a balloon that's collapsed at rest, but is really big when it has to be, during birth.

The woman's contribution to "It Takes Two, Baby" starts farther in, on the other end of the fallopian tubes (see, they do have *some* tubes), so let's go there now.

That contribution is the egg. If you have a daughter, she'll have about 1 million eggs at birth, although none of them start maturing until much later. Unlike a male, she doesn't produce any more eggs during her lifetime; she just brings them to maturation (in the years between puberty and menopause) usually one at a time each month. While an egg is no larger than a dot on this page, it's the biggest cell in the human body.

Immature eggs hang out in follicles inside an ovary. There's one ovary on each side of a female—right under the point halfway between the top of her leg and her belly button. The two ovaries also generate female hormones like estrogen that facilitate the menstruation and pregnancy cycles.

These hormones stimulate the follicles, and each month an egg matures, cuts loose, and gets pushed out of the ovary. Close to the opening of each ovary is a fallopian tube, which can snag the egg, and muscle it along a 3.5-inch circular path to the uterus. There is one fallopian tube for each ovary.

If a sperm and an egg get together, they'll do it in a fallopian tube (a wonderfully romantic name, huh?). The successful sperm passes through the wall of the egg cell, fertilizes it, and we're off to the zygote races.

Saving Private Sperm

When you ejaculate, you send out hundreds of sperm. But before you start thinking too highly of yourself (or your sperm) for generating such huge numbers each time, remember this: Sperm are a lot like lemmings.

Most of the time, none of the sperm will reach a fertile female egg. Your sperms' cumulative batting average wouldn't even qualify for a Little League team.

But that one time when a sperm makes solid contact with an egg is called conception, the start of a miraculous chain reaction. You can get a positive pregnancy tests as early as 7 to 10 days after conception, even before your partner notices that she's missed a period.

Crib Notes _____

> The combined sperm and egg are called the zygote. All of the genetic information and material your baby will ever have is there in the zygote right from the beginning, even though it's only about one tenth of a millimeter long.

Egg on the Wall

Within a couple weeks, the zygote has been pushed down the fallopian tube into the uterus (there's pushing involved right from the beginning!). If a number of things progress exactly according to plan, the zygote then attaches itself to the endometrium, a lush lining of tissue and blood along the wall of the uterus. (If no zygote attaches to the endometrium, it deteriorates and is flushed out of the uterus each month—in the process known as menstruation, or "having a period.")

Once the zygote latches onto the uterine wall, pregnancy begins. From now on, what used to be the zygote is called an embryo. There's often confusion about terms like *embryo* and *fetus*. During pregnancy, an embryo remains an embryo until all of its major organs have developed, and then we call it a fetus (or *foetus*, if you're British).

The "Normal" Schedule Inside the Womb

By about **one month** after conception, scientists can start to detect a head on the embryo, with a primitive brain and spinal cord. Soon afterward, lungs begin their earliest development, and the heartbeat starts.

OB/GYN

Determining what week you're in during your pregnancy is an inexact science. Partly that is due to the fact that doctors can't really know with certainty when you conceived, so there isn't a firm date from which to start counting forward. Partly it's due to the fact that different embryos and fetuses develop at slightly different rates.

In the **second month,** the pace picks up as the embryo grows organs that will eventually turn into eyes, legs, liver, arms, elbows, and facial features. The embryo starts to move, but the limbs are so tiny that their movement is imperceptible to the mother.

If you could climb inside the womb with a microscope during **month three,** you'd see the embryo's intestines growing—but on the outside, since there isn't room for them inside yet. You'd also see asexual genitalia, and the beginnings of a facial profile. By the end of the month, you probably would see the transition from embryo to fetus, because all the major organs are getting in place.

During **month four,** the fetus starts swallowing, urinating, and growing fingernails. The intestines move inside, now that the abdomen has room, and vocal chords are springing up. A doctor may even be able to detect a heartbeat, using a fetal monitor.

The **fifth month** brings toenails and, in girls, the development of ovaries (with enough eggs to repeat this whole process some years down the road). The fetus also starts moving her eyes slowly, and can begin coordinating the movement of her ever-growing limbs. The head is still much larger than the rest of the body, but the difference is narrowing.

By the beginning of **month six,** many mothers can feel "quickening"—a vague sense that something's moving in there—or else actually perceptible movement. Some women say it's like air or a water balloon inside them. Boys will develop testes and girls their vagina and uterus. The fetus may start hiccupping, and will grow eyebrows along with other fine body hair.

In **month seven,** the fetus' hearing has improved to the point that he can hear his mother's organs at work (how scientists know this is beyond me, but they do). The growth of his brain really takes off. By this time, the lungs, while still not nearly developed, have grown enough so that the fetus could survive (with tons of medical attention) if he were born.

During the **eighth month,** the fetus' eyes are open, with eyelids to help, and she may begin to suck her thumb. Fat is building up under her skin, and she can surpass 5 pounds in weight (if she's in there alone). She may start having predictable sleep patterns, but will be moving so much when awake, that you should have no trouble feeling (and maybe seeing) the movement on your partner's belly. She may now be able to distinguish different sounds—including your voice (so, talk to her!!!).

By the **ninth month,** the baby is normally head down in the uterus, and plumb out of space. With no room to kick, he'll wiggle and squirm instead. Brain growth continues at warp speed, more fat and weight are packed on, and by the end of the month, he may "drop" down into mom's pelvis in preparation to leave (putting a lot of pressure on mom's bladder). His fingernails have already grown full length, and he starts to scratch himself (no, it's not just boys who scratch themselves, girls do it, too!).

In the **tenth month,** all parties have probably lost patience. Yes, Papa, there can be a tenth month, although what seems like the tenth month may just be a case of the doctor miscalculating your conception date. Remember that the normal "term" of a pregnancy falls between 38 and 40 weeks from the first day of conception. That's a fairly wide window to begin with, and a baby occasionally stays in there beyond 40 weeks.

The key word at this point is *patience*. Your baby is still growing like a weed (a pattern most babies follow for years after they finally pop out). Bottom line: She's not going to stay in there.

This brings us to the end of perhaps the shortest summary of womb-life on record. See Appendix B for books that can give you a lot more detail. Plus, if your doctor is worth her salt, she'll be telling you plenty as things go along.

I liked knowing as much as I could about how the baby was developing inside my wife's uterus. (Until the day our twins were born, we were under the delusion that there was only one baby in there.) That information helped me imagine what was happening to the baby, and helped me start bonding with her/them long before her/their birthday.

However, I have to admit, I spent a lot more time during our pregnancy concentrating on and trying to cope with the host of changes (many of them unpredictable) going on with my wife. All of Chapter 4 is dedicated to this challenge. But once you know what an intense and wild growth ride the baby takes from egg to exit, it's easier to understand why a woman is on a wild ride herself, with all this underway inside her.

The Least You Need to Know

- Male and female reproductive organs are miraculous, but don't have to be mysterious. Make sure you know how they work.
- Conception starts when a sperm fertilizes an egg, forming a zygote. Pregnancy starts when the zygote attaches to the uterine wall and becomes an embryo. The embryo becomes a fetus once all the major organs are formed, usually by month four.

- Precision and pregnancy seldom share the same sentence. Don't get too hung up on due dates or what month you think you're in, because no one can say with absolute certainty when you conceived.

- Knowing the approximate growth and development of your soon-to-be-baby is exciting and fun. It also helps build the crucial father-child bond that you and your child will need the rest of your lives.

Chapter 3

A Man's First Trip to the Gynecologist

In This Chapter

- Choosing your OB/GYN
- How the OB/GYN helps you
- Midwives, doulas, and "alternative" methods
- Making yourself heard and involved

Chances are you've yet to have your first appointment with a gynecologist. If you're that rare guy who has accompanied your partner to a gynecologist, then you know how valuable your support of your partner and your advocacy for her treatment are.

When you find out you're expecting, the two of you need to choose a doctor or nurse-midwife who has experience delivering babies. Most of the time, this will be a gynecologist who is also an obstetrician, or if you're using a midwife, she'll be a certified nurse-midwife. Many family practice doctors or general practitioners also oversee a woman's pregnancy and deliver babies. However, they always have an OB/GYN on call in case complications arise. To keep things simple, I'll use the term *OB/GYN* for the doctor, even if he or she may not be a specialist.

He or she *will* be your primary resource on the health of your partner and your soon-to-be-baby. The OB/GYN may be the doctor your partner already has been seeing for her annual pap smears, or it may be someone entirely new.

Either way, it's important for you to participate in choosing your OB/GYN and to participate in your partner's health care up to and beyond the day of birth.

 Crib Notes

A gynecologist is a medical doctor (M.D.) or doctor of osteopathy (D.O.) who specializes in treating and preventing sexual and reproductive health problems in women.

An obstetrician is a gynecologist who dedicates all or part of his or her practice to treating pregnant women and delivering babies.

A perinatologist is an obstetrician who specializes in treating women with special medical problems during pregnancy, due to her heredity, chronic illnesses, or other factors.

Why *You* Need to Go to the OB/GYN

Why should you go to the OB/GYN? You can sum-
marize the main reason in one short sentence: Because this is your (plural) pregnancy.

Don't Touch My Wife!

Now, you may not be crazy about your partner going
to a gynecologist, period. After all, there's a perfect
stranger (sometimes a man) peering and poking into
her genitalia, ordering mammograms, and who
knows what else!

I have news for you. If you talk to a gynecologist
outside business hours, nearly every one (regardless
of whether it's a man or a woman doctor) will tell
you that any titillation there might have been in a
pelvic examination is long gone by the time you
leave medical school. Looking into a "stranger's"
vagina quickly looses sexual allure when you do it
120 times a week, every week.

Pregnant Pauses

> Having been through two deliveries of
> babies, I can only say this about them:
> Go where the road takes you and stay
> on top of the wave. The adrenaline rush
> through the whole thing is amazing, and
> it's the best high in the world, be it natural
> or artificial.
> —Doug

The first step in preparing to visit the OB/GYN with your partner is to toss fear and jealousy overboard.

You're Pregnant, Too

This pregnancy is bringing major changes to your life. Some of the changes are obvious, and others will take some time (maybe years) to fully understand. You might make radical modifications in your own behavior. This father's story is a perfect example:

> I told my wife I would quit smoking as soon as she became pregnant. On a Friday I came home and she showed me the pregnancy test. I was speechless. I quit smoking (the single hardest thing I have ever done) the following Sunday. On Wednesday of the next week she miscarried. But because I now knew we could get pregnant, I did not pick up a cigarette the day she miscarried despite her telling me to do what I needed to do. It's been 5 years and 2 beautiful little girls, and I still am not smoking.

The transformation from man to father is stressful, no matter how excited you are by the prospect. You have tons of questions, no previous experience (if this is your first time), and intense desires to protect your baby and your partner.

A great antidote to that stress is information, which an OB/GYN has plenty of. Another antidote is confidence that someone is looking out for your partner. A good OB/GYN does that, too.

So there are some selfish reasons for an expectant father to develop a good working relationship with the OB/GYN. But a more important reason to do so is your partner.

Regardless of whether your partner has had a baby before (and especially if she hasn't) she needs every ounce of moral support you can give her. Going with her to the doctor is tangible support she can see and feel.

Plus, there's the practical benefit. It's a little hard to keep mentally sharp when someone is examining your cervix, or hooking up medical equipment for tests. With all that going on, it's easy for an expectant mom to forget some of the questions she wanted to ask her OB/GYN, or some important information she wanted to pass along. That's where you come in.

When you're in the doctor's office, concentrate on two things:

- **Giving your partner the support she needs.** Be upbeat and cheer her on, even if you've been waiting in the examination room for a half hour.

- **Advocating with and for her.** Make sure the doctor answers all of her questions—and yours. If you've been waiting in the examination room for a half hour, be the one who goes and finds out why.

The last, best reason for going to every OB/GYN appointment is how it engages you in the pregnancy. A lot of what's happening in the pregnancy is abstract to the expectant father—certainly more abstract than to your partner, who is getting her belly kicked from the inside out.

OB/GYN

Use a notebook to write down questions you've gathered (and want answered) since your last OB/GYN appointment, and information you want to pass along. Things like:

- Are there any more comfortable ways for her to sleep at night?
- Over the last couple of weeks, she's been experiencing *(fill in the blank)*. Is that normal?

Bring the notebook with you and make sure you get satisfactory answers to all of your questions. Use the notebook to write down the answers, too, so you don't forget the information when you get back home.

Being part of the OB/GYN world makes things more real for you, and helps you prepare psychologically. You'll probably have your first look at the baby as a grainy, swimming image on the doctor's sonogram machine. You'll hear the baby's heartbeat a lot sooner if you have the doctor's stethoscope.

But you can't experience any of that if you don't show up. And one of the first rules of fathering is: Show up.

Your First Visit

If you have to miss any OB/GYN appointment, do *not* miss the first one, because it's probably the most important. This visit is usually longer than the others, but that's because the doctor needs to get a medical history (if he or she doesn't already have one) and assess your partner's health and health risks.

You'll get asked (both of you) whether you've had any sexually transmitted diseases, been exposed recently to contagious diseases like measles, and whether you smoke. Your partner will need to tell about previous medical problems, what drugs she's taking (both prescription and over-the-counter).

The OB/GYN will want to know whether you or your partner have a family history of chronic illness or genetic abnormalities. For instance, if there's a history of Down syndrome, muscular dystrophy, or spina bifida, the doctor will more aggressively watch for signs during the pregnancy. You'll also be asked about diseases common to your ethnic background, like sickle cell anemia in African Americans.

You can *ask* questions, too. Of course you'll want to know your due date and how far along your pregnancy seems to be. You might also want to ask about diet and nutrition, exercise, what symptoms are normal, whether your partner is at risk for any problems during pregnancy, and so on.

This is one doctor's visit when you want to be sure to write down your list of questions the night before. In the excitement of "our first appointment," it's easy to forget some of the things you were sure you were going to ask. This visit is also the time to ask "Who do I call in your office when we have questions between appointments?"

Giving the Compatibility Test

Do we want a traditional doctor or hospital for our pregnancy and delivery?

This is another one of these communication challenges you face as a couple. (Remember, these "dry runs" help you practice how you'll communicate when raising the kids.) When deciding on an OB/GYN and hospital, you'll have to communicate clearly with each other and with the prospective providers you interview.

Dads and Dollars

Nowadays, insurance coverage (including government medical coverage) can add red tape to choosing a doctor. Find out ahead of time from the insurer which clinics and doctors are covered by your plan. Also, read the fine print of your policy and/or push a customer service rep to see if the company will cover doctors outside their "group"—and what criteria they use to approve that move.

Your marital status can also play a big role. Some insurers put limitations on coverage or availability of policies if the parents-to-be aren't married.

Yes, if you can, you should interview prospective OB/GYNs and hospitals. So don't be timid about it.

Finding the Right OB/GYN

Picking an OB/GYN is kind of like picking a roommate at school. You'll spend a fair amount of time together over the next nine months, the most intense being at the very end (finals at school, labor at the hospital). Like a roommate, your OB/GYN doesn't necessarily have to be the kind of person you'd marry. On the other hand, he or she shouldn't be the kind of person you despise.

Basically, you want to find someone with whom you are compatible. Someone who understands, respects (and perhaps shares) your values. Someone you can communicate with.

You also want to be aware of what kind of people you and your partner are—and not let other people railroad you into what they think is best. If you like being in charge and think the doctor should be more of a colleague than anything else, fine. If you think that, because the doctor went to med school, we should leave all the decisions in his hands, that's fine, too—as long as it suits what you need.

Find a physician and hospital (or birthing center) who believe in your perspective and will work with and for you—with the ultimate goal of having a healthy baby.

The Cleveland Clinic suggests some very practical questions to ask when seeking a health-care provider for your pregnancy (or anything else, for that matter). Here are a few:

- How long have you been in practice?
- When and where did you receive training?
- Are you board-certified? Do you have references?
- Have you had any problems with your medical practice? (To get this information, contact your state medical licensing board.)
- What is your philosophy about pregnancy, labor, and delivery? (Think about how that fits in with your own beliefs.)
- How many babies do you deliver per week?
- How many children do you have?
- Are you in a group practice? If so, do we have a choice about whom we see and who delivers our baby?
- Will you be in town around our due date? (No one doctor is awake and available 24/7, so be sure you know which colleague(s) might end up delivering your baby—and make sure those colleagues know what you want when the time comes.)
- If we have a question, who do we call? Who responds to the calls? Do you accept questions via e-mail?
- Will you respect our personal birth plan? (More on birthing plans in Chapter 6.)
- Do you induce labor if we go beyond our due date?
- Can and will you deliver the baby in the facility we want to use?

- How do you feel about working with a midwife and/or doula (more on those later)?

You may worry that a trained, professional doctor will be insulted by this kind of interrogation. But in fact, most doctors are used to having people ask these questions. Be aware of *how* the doctor answers your questions (body language, tone of voice, etc.) as well as the words of the answers. Look for someone you can negotiate with over the nine months of pregnancy. If you trust the doctor's style, that's a real plus.

If, on the other hand, the prospective OB/GYN says or acts like he or she is insulted by your questions, then thank him or her for his or her time—and find another doctor!

Dr. Joy Dorscher, who delivers dozens of babies each year, says, "When you get right down to it, parents don't really need me there most of the time; nature knows how to deliver a baby. But when they *do* need me (because baby or mother are in trouble), then they *really* need me." Dorscher's philosophy for working with expectant parents is simple: "I'll do everything you want as long as I can, but then you need to let me do what I need to do when I have to do it. That's my job."

Some veteran parents (and even some doctors and nurses) suggest that you get recommendations from the nursing staff at the hospital you're using. Those nurses see the doctors at peak stress times, and know which ones are best at listening to and respecting what the expectant couple wants. That makes nurses very good sources.

Where Do We Birth This Baby?

No, most babies are not born in the back seat of a cab during a blizzard (stop watching so many sitcoms!). Besides, it's really hard to boil water in a cab (why do they need all that boiling water anyway?)

However, you don't necessarily have to go to a hospital to have a baby nowadays. There are birthing centers—and even that millennia-old birth locale: home. But hospitals are still far and away the most common place for a birth.

The process for choosing a place for your baby's birth is very much like the process of choosing a OB/GYN. Ask *a lot* of questions. First, ask yourself:

- If I'm not thrilled with the hospital where our OB/GYN delivers babies, is it worth finding another doctor?
- Can we get to the hospital quickly and easily?
- Do we want to have the baby somewhere other than a hospital?

We'll turn to the experts at the Cleveland Clinic again for a list of questions to ask the hospital and/or your doctor about what you want on the big day:

- Where does our doctor normally deliver babies? Does he or she have privileges at other hospitals?
- Will our insurance cover treatment at this hospital?
- When can we take a tour of the hospital?

- What are your procedures when a woman arrives in labor?

- Is there an anesthesiologist on duty? (If you need the anesthesiologist for surgery or pain relief, you'd rather not wait while he or she drives to work.)

- What is the nurse to patient ratio? The American College of OB/GYNs recommends one nurse per two women during early labor, and one nurse per woman in the pushing stage.

- Does the hospital have perinatologists or neonatologists (doctors who specialize in treating preterm babies) on staff?

- Can I spend the night in the room with my partner after delivery? What type of sleeping arrangements will I have?

- Does the hospital allow the baby to stay with us in our room? If so, can we still go to the nursery if we need help with feeding, getting the baby to sleep, etc.?

- Does the hospital have a one-room option (labor, delivery, and recovery all in the same room)?

- Are water births done here?

- Is there access to a whirlpool/tub for women in labor?

- What is the hospital's rate of doing cesarean sections and administering epidurals?

- Can the two of us be together at all times, including in the operating room, if we have a cesarean delivery?

- Can our other children attend the birth?
- Is video taping allowed during delivery?
- Does the hospital have a "new family" class or other resources to teach us how to care for our newborn?
- When can family and friends visit? Can children visit?
- Is parking close? Is it free? (This is something you don't want to research when your partner is doubled over in the car with contractions.)

Crib Notes

Surgeons perform a cesarean section (C-section for short) when the baby can't be born safely through the birth canal. They cut through the abdomen and into the uterus, pull the baby out, and then sew Mom back up. This takes a much larger toll on Mom's body (and sometimes the baby), adding substantially to recovery time.

An epidural is the injection of medicine into a part of the spinal column called the epidural space (hence the name). The injection itself may be painful, but the goal is to numb the pain a mother feels in the last stages of labor.

As you can see, there are a lot of options and a lot of decisions to make—it's a good thing you have nine months to talk about it all!

Doing the Doula and Other Birthing Alternatives

There are too many health-care options for pregnancy and childbirth to do justice to them here. There are tons of books and websites about pregnancy and birthing options (see Appendix B for some). Many of these have large blind spots when it comes to expectant fathers (although that's slowly improving). Their information is often aimed exclusively at the pregnant woman, but you can still read and learn from it.

Here's a very quick, scratch-the-surface look at some common "alternative birth" terms and people.

Midwifery

Try saying *midwifery* out loud. You can't do it without feeling like you mispronounced it! It also sounds like some ancient and mysterious craft lost to history.

Well, midwifery is ancient, but it's not mysterious or lost to history. One of today's most common "alternative" ways of giving birth is to use a certified nurse-midwife (CNM) as your primary caregiver, instead of a medical doctor.

CNMs are Master's-degree registered nurses with specialized training (and state licenses) in obstetrics. Most work with hospitals, and have a network of anesthesiologists, neonatologists, and OB/GYNs to call on if complications arise.

Nurse-midwives tend to be less formal and more family centered in their philosophy than a traditional OB/GYN. If there aren't complications or high risks in the pregnancy, CNMs can be an excellent way to go. The American College of Nurse-Midwives has a lot of information at www.acnm.org or 202-728-9860.

Some midwives are not nurses and/or are not certified. While these midwives may have a lot of experience, insurance companies are not likely to pay for their services. Also, in many locations, physicians cannot work with them because of liability issues.

Birth Centers

Birth Centers or Birthing Centers are homelike facilities, often near a hospital, and sometimes inside one. They are usually cheaper than a hospital, and proponents say the birth center approach cuts down on the number of C-sections. According to the National Association of Childbearing Centers, they use a "wellness" model of pregnancy and birth. In other words, it's an approach that emphasizes that childbirth is natural and not a disease.

Because they are more homelike, birth centers tend to be more family friendly—for example, there's seldom a problem with other children and relatives being present for labor and delivery. They are often staffed by nurse-midwives.

And, like nurse-midwives, birth centers are regulated by states, and accredited by the Commission for the Accreditation of Birth Centers. (I mean, who else would do it?) They also draw on a network of specialists if complications arise, and since they are close to a hospital, they can get you there quickly if need be. Find out more at www.birthcenters.org, 215-234-8068, or by e-mailing ReachNACC@ BirthCenters.org.

Doula, Doobie-Doo

No, doula is not the title of a doo-wop song. It's an ancient Greek word that refers to a woman who is experienced with labor, and gives emotional and physical support to a pregnant woman and her partner during labor, delivery, and afterward.

She is not a medical professional, but is trained to provide things to ease the discomfort of pregnancy and labor—like massage, aromatherapy, and the comfort of wisdom and knowledge drawn from past experience. In other words, she fills the role played for centuries by older female relatives and neighbors.

University of Toronto nursing Professor Dr. Ellen D. Hodnett studied 13,000 pregnant women and found that those using the support of nonmedical companions like doulas had fewer complications during labor, and were less likely to need epidurals or C-sections.

Dr. Hodnett says:

> The organization of care in modern [hospital] maternity units—including shift changes, diverse staff responsibilities, and staff shortages— appears to limit the effectiveness of labor sup- port provided by members of the hospital staff.

Nonhospital caregivers may be able to give greater attention to the mothers' needs.

Doulas emphasize support for the father and mother both; for example, using their knowledge to help ease fathers' anxiety in the intense hours of labor and delivery. You can get more information from the Doulas of North America at www.dona.org, 1-888-788-3662, or e-mail Doula@DONA.org.

Listen to Daddy: Participating in the Process and Making Yourself Heard

Being an expectant father is like being a knight of the round table. You have to be strong, but you also have to know when to use your strength—and when to use your gentleness or powers of persuasion instead.

If a woman reaches a curb where a large, muddy puddle lies, you lay down your cape so she can cross without soiling her feet. But, you don't tell her which street to cross, or when. You fight for your beloved's honor, but never forget that your beloved's honor belongs to her.

Reading through this chapter, you've seen many places where your opinion can count, where you can participate in making decisions, and where your support can make this shared pregnancy the most amazing experience possible.

OB/GYN

- Your level of participation in the pregnancy shows your level of commitment to your partner and baby—something your partner will be highly attuned to.

- Don't put up with being treated like a fifth wheel, but be polite about it.

- Don't tolerate your partner being ignored or disrespected by a caregiver, but (guess what?) be polite about it.

- You can never *really* change someone's mind with yelling, threats, or violence. So throw those "tools" away.

- Speak up for what you think is best, and always be open to compromise—especially with your partner. After all, it's her body that will ultimately deliver the baby.

- When it comes to your partner and your primary caregiver, communicate, communicate, and then, communicate some more.

For example, the hospital staff may be very busy right when your partner decides she wants some pain relief during labor. Your job is to go find your partner's primary doctor or nurse and get the situation addressed right away. Like in most human relationships, it is not effective to get into the doctor's face and scream, "Where the hell have you been?!?" Rudeness is ineffective, so be polite and firm.

But also be aware of things you can let slide or do for yourself. For example, don't make a federal case to the hospital staff if you run out of ice chips. Ask where the ice machine is, and get more on your own (you might need to take a little walk occasionally for your mental health anyway).

Just like a medieval knight, when you advocate for yourself and your partner, you have to know your boundaries and choose your battles wisely. With that in mind, here are a few things to remember.

The Least You Need to Know

- You're allowed to pick doctors, hospitals, and other health-care providers with whom you are compatible.
- When it comes to pregnancy and birth, the only stupid question is the one you don't ask.
- There are many options for your labor and delivery, so do what you can to get the ones you want.
- You are your partner's chief advocate from pregnancy through delivery and beyond.

Chapter 4

Is This the Woman I Married?

In This Chapter

- Making sense of her moods (and yours)
- Caring for her (and yourself)
- Enjoying the good stuff
- Will sex hurt the baby?

You're an expectant father. The "expectant" part means that you can't see your baby-to-be until delivery, so there isn't much concrete, observable phenomena to hang your hat on. However, you *can* see your partner, and she has more than enough observable phenomena to keep you hopping.

Hormones rule pregnancy. Hormones, emotions, and psychology rule a pregnant woman, and it's sometimes hard to tell where one starts and another begins. Remember (as mentioned in Chapter 1), that *you* also have new levels of hormones, emotions, and psychology coursing through you.

During your pregnancy, all these factors will create what looks like (and often is) chaos. Believe it or not, this chaos can bring you and your partner closer together, provided you know how to respond.

There Is No "Normal"

Inside your partner's uterus, the baby is undergoing rapid physical growth and change. Your partner is going through both interior and exterior physical change, too. Her belly is getting bigger, her skin may change tint, her breasts may get larger, and so on.

But the impact of what's going inside her emotions and thought process will have a *much* greater impact on your daily life. Unfortunately, it's harder to predict the timing of those emotions and thought processes than it is to predict the physical development of a fetus.

Some women have meltdown crying jags every day in the third month, while others have them during the eighth month. Some women have them in both months (and every month in between) and others never have any. There's no surefire "normal" pattern to what a woman will feel as she progresses through pregnancy. Nor is there one paint-by-the-numbers way for a man to experience his partner's pregnancy.

But never fear! You are in luck. In fact, as the expectant dad, you are in a better position than anyone else to make this time satisfying and even fun. You are also in the best position to help pregnancy deepen your relationship with your partner and your new child. That requires some awareness and work, as you're about to learn.

Her, You, and What to Do

While there is no "normal" for a pregnant couple, there are things that a lot of expectant parents do tend to experience in month three versus month eight.

This next section is a brief, scratch-the-surface rundown of what you might expect from and in your partner and yourself month-by-month. (See Appendix B for great resources that give you as much detail as you'd ever need.) Keep in mind: If you don't see or feel things in this order, that doesn't necessarily mean anything is wrong.

First I'll explain what may be going on with her, then what may be going on with you. Then, equally (if not more) important, you'll learn what you can do to squeeze every good thing from this amazing time in your lives. So say it out loud: "Her, you, what to do. Her, you, what to do." Say it in rhythm, and you can cha-cha along!

Pregnant Pauses

As soon as you find out you're expecting, start searching for veteran dads. An experienced father can answer a question, even if it strikes you as a bit silly. Find a man you can share your anxiety, panic, and uncertainty with. You'll be amazed how much better you'll feel—and how much smarter you'll be.

Month One

Her: Chances are that for most (if not all) of the first month, she may not even know that she's pregnant. If she does find out, then she'll probably feel bursts of general excitement and anxiety. The feelings may be more intense in her than in you (as they may be throughout early pregnancy), because all of the physical changes she is anticipating in and to her body.

Your partner may also be a bit cranky; if her mood gets touchy before getting her period each month, this will look familiar.

You: You're likely to feel a bit excited and a bit panicked. You may wonder if you can afford a baby, or whether you want to stay in this romantic relationship. You may wonder what you got yourself into. But your feelings may not be as intense as your partner's right now. Why not?

Many an expectant dad says that in the early months, the pregnancy didn't seem as real to him as it did to her. In fact, pregnancy is a more "abstract" concept for the man at the beginning, because he can't even see any physical change in his partner yet.

What to do: Start living by the mantra: Communicate, communicate, communicate. Listen to her. Encourage her excitement and understand her anxiety. Find a good time to share some of your anxieties with her—"strong and silent" does not win this race.

But make sure you share *all* of your excitement and pride with her, too. Tell her how beautiful she is and what a miracle this is. On the practical front, start screening health-care professionals for your pregnancy and delivery. Then, *go to the doctor with her!*

To prevent birth defects, make sure she takes folic acid daily and completely abstains from alcohol use as soon as you find out you are pregnant. Review each and every other drug she takes (even over-the-counter ones) with her doctor.

Month Two

Her: Your partner may feel physically tired over the first few months, as her body adjusts to pregnancy. Emotionally, she's probably going to be feeling the same range of feelings—and crankiness, too—as she did last month. Physically, there may be more tangible evidence of her pregnancy. The one you'll hear most about is *morning sickness*.

Crib Notes

Misnamed **morning sickness** happens at any time of day or night. While more common in early months, it can last throughout the pregnancy. It is nausea that frequently involves vomiting triggered by smells of certain food or other odors. Not all women get morning sickness, but if it comes, you have to make sure Mom gets enough fluids, vitamins, and nutrition to replace what she's upchucking. Your OB/GYN or midwife will have strategies and/or medications to use.

Food is a key factor in a pregnant woman's life. She may start having cravings. My wife had been a vegetarian for years, and suddenly craved steak. The key thing is making sure to get the full menu of nutrition and vitamins, because she is eating for two.

You: You may start having mood swings and bouts of crankiness yourself. It's normal to charge back and forth between euphoria and the blues. If feelings of depression hang on without letup, however, see *your* physician for guidance.

Month two usually brings the first tests of your patience. She is getting harder to predict, and you have to accept that fact—while also doing your best to pick up on the cues she's giving about how she's feeling. Practice your patience. It's like a muscle that gets stronger with exercise, and you'll have to exercise it a lot the next few months (and years).

What you can do: Unless the physician objects, go with your partner's food cravings. They may change rapidly; something she craved last week may spark nausea today. Keep talking and listening. If it starts to feel like you're riding a roller coaster, remember how thrilling a real roller coaster is, and that each dip comes before a hill.

Month Three

Her: She may still act like she has chronic PMS, but she also may have moments of calm about the pregnancy. It seems like she's urinating every five minutes because the growing uterus is starting to pressure her bladder (it'll get worse as the uterus gets really big).

Other parts of her digestion may be giving her fits, too: nausea, constipation, gas (remember to use polite terms in polite company, boys), bloating, and heartburn. She may get weary and sleepy more easily, have headaches, or even get dizzy or faint. She's also starting to grow out of her clothes by month three or four.

You: As she becomes more visibly pregnant, the reality may start closing in on you. This can trigger more rounds of emotional reactions (perhaps more intense than previously) of joy and fear. You may also feel sexually frustrated. Nausea and vomiting are not very romantic, so you may have trouble getting on the same sexual schedule, or any at all.

Remember that this situation is temporary and not a reason to do something stupid (or should we say *really stupid*) like playing the blame game or looking for sexual "satisfaction" elsewhere. In fact, now is an ideal opportunity to explore the other aspects of intimacy: verbal, emotional, and spiritual. These not only make your relationship richer (and your parenting more fun), but they generally have a marvelous effect on the sex, once that mode of intimacy returns.

What you can do: Lead the nutrition initiative. Make sure both of you are eating healthy, balanced meals—and completely avoiding dangerous substances like alcohol, smoking, illicit drugs, pesticides, etc. Go shopping with her to pick out relaxed, easy to use (and easy to wash, since you'll be doing more laundry) clothes. Keep telling her how beautiful she is because she is probably starting to have that special glow (and because she needs to hear you say it).

OB/GYN

Smoking, alcohol, and illicit drugs are poison to your baby, before and after birth. It's exponentially harder for a pregnant woman to stop using these chemicals if her partner keeps on using them (besides which, it's not fair to her). So stop now.

Every state and most insurance companies have smoking cessation programs—these greatly improve the odds of kicking a habit that will always endanger your child (kids living with secondhand smoke are far more likely to get asthma). Use them.

If you or your partner have difficulty giving up alcohol or other drugs, even when the stakes are as high as they are in pregnancy, then you may need help in this department, too. Millions of people misuse alcohol and/or other drugs, so you're not alone if you develop this problem. Even more fortunate, millions of people recover with the right help. Look in the Yellow Pages under alcohol or drug treatment. Or access these organizations for free information:

- National Institute on Alcohol Abuse and Alcoholism at www.niaaa.nih. gov/faq/faq.htm

- National Organization on Fetal Alcohol Syndrome at www. nofas.org or 1-800-66-NOFAS

- National Clearinghouse for Alcohol and Drug Information at www. health.org
- Alcoholics Anonymous at www. aa.org or 212-870-3400

Addiction wrecks families, so there's every reason in the world to act now if you have trouble with booze or drugs. Your kids will thank you for it, and *your* life will be a lot more healthy and happy.

Month Four

Her: She may feel the baby move by now. People are noticing she's pregnant, including friends and/ or perfect strangers who want to share "when we were pregnant" stories and compulsively rub their hands over her belly. She may start being scatter-brained, feeling forgetful and disorganized. She may also start getting impatient for this all to be over, even though you're not even halfway home.

Physically, most women see an end to morning sickness around now, although they can still be constipated, flatulent, and need to pee more often than anyone thought possible. Most women now have noticeably larger breasts, as they swell to pre-pare for feeding the baby. Varicose veins and swollen feet often start showing up now, too—and she's liable to still be sleepier than usual.

You: Many men start to feel "sympathy pains" by this point, echoing the more obvious symptoms their partners are feeling. Don't let anyone tell you that this is weird or ridiculous. Your hormones are changing during this pregnancy—and you're liable to instinctively tune in to your partner's moods. Naturally, this tends to put your moods into a swing, too.

Your partner will sense the baby move inside her before you can feel it. It's easy to feel left out when she gets that excitement and you don't. Be patient, you'll soon be able to feel the kicks through her belly.

What you can do: Be a coach and cheerleader. When your partner gets impatient, reassure her and show her that you're going to be there through thick and thin (so don't go out with the boys every time she's moody). Be as protective as she wants you to be; play the "bad cop" if she needs a break from other people's horror stories or getting her belly patted by strangers.

If you're feeling a bit left out, ask your partner to describe in detail what she feels the baby doing, use your imagination, and share her excitement. Some days, she'll be so preoccupied with her body that you'll need to find someone else to talk to about your own concerns. Make use of those veteran dads all around you.

Month Five

Her: Backache city. The fast-growing fetus is starting to put plenty of strain on her body, with swollen and/or cramping feet and legs, and achy joints. There may be slight changes in the color and texture of her skin and nipples, and her gums may bleed when she brushes her teeth (all normal). Her vagina may discharge small amounts of a white fluid. That's called leukorrhea; it can last all through pregnancy (also normal). Plus, her belly button has probably become an "outie."

She may have a monster appetite, now that nausea has gone adios. Many women also experience a hearty sexual appetite during the second trimester, and may achieve orgasm more easily than usual.

You: You may be feeding off of her sexual appetite and relishing every minute of it. Increased sexual desire during pregnancy is natural (for instance, you don't have to worry about getting pregnant!). Unless your physician says there's a medical reason to avoid intercourse (there usually isn't), go for it. Contrary to what you might have heard, it doesn't hurt the baby. If, for medical reasons, intercourse isn't an option, indulge in alternative ways to satisfy each other's libido.

On the other hand, your respective libidos may be on opposite schedules, or seem completely deflated. Your partner may now be striking you as more maternal than sexual, which can be confusing. This is fairly common, and in most cases, this will pass.

What you can do: On the libido front, follow your partner's lead. It may feel a bit awkward at first to have intercourse when the baby is in there, too. You'll get over that, though, and have the chance for some great sex. With or without intercourse, you can make your intimacy warm, engaged, cuddly, affectionate, passionate, and mysteriously different than before.

Be willing to try different positions for intercourse and other sexual contact. Alternative ways of touching, showing affection, and communicating can keep you close to each other—and perhaps bring you closer than before. No matter what the scenario, take advantage of the opportunity for greater intimacy (spiritual, emotional, and physical). Nature is helping you out here.

Encourage her food appetite, but make sure it stays balanced (she can't have fast-food triple cheeseburgers for every meal). Embrace the opportunity to try new cuisine, but be aware that some foods (like sushi and other raw fish) are now off limits. However, spicy food is just fine, if it doesn't upset her stomach. Most important, follow your physician's guidelines.

Month Six

Her: By this time, your partner might be sick and tired of all the folderol, can't believe there's three more months to go, or at the very least, wants people to quit bugging her about expecting.

It's natural to feel impatient and/or bored when you have to urinate every few minutes and struggle to fit behind the steering wheel. Many physical symptoms she's been feeling may continue right through to the end. She also might get hemorrhoids, nosebleeds, and/or congestion of the ears and sinuses. Fun stuff, no?

You: You may be wondering whether your relationship with your partner will ever be the same again. The answer is yes and no. Many of the central things that drew you together will always remain. Plus, if you take full advantage of all these new experiences (and remember to communicate, communicate, communicate), your relationship will be *better* than ever.

There may be days this month (or any month) when you think that you won't be a great father. You might worry that you'll have the same shortcomings as your own dad or that you just don't have the disposition or capacity for the job. Those worries are normal, so don't let them paralyze you.

You may start dreaming about your child-to-be. The details of the dream (like her gender) aren't predictive or as important as the deep bond you're beginning to form with her. I dreamt several times of seeing my two children from behind. The older, taller one had an arm around the younger one's shoulder, while they looked over a wooden fence into a farm field. It was very cool, but clearly not predictive (we had twins in downtown Omaha).

What you can do: Rub her feet, back, legs, and anyplace else that feels good to her. Follow her lead on the intensity of your massage technique; doing it too hard or too soft may make her feel worse. Even if your massage doesn't relieve the pain, it provides comfort, which she needs a lot of now.

Work to nurture your relationship with your partner. It's necessary and calming. Plus, it's good practice. If you think the distractions of pregnancy challenge partner-partner bonds, wait until there are kids underfoot! Now and in the future, it's important to make space and time for your relationship, so get in the habit now.

Sign up for an infant CPR (cardio-pulmonary resuscitation) class. You may never ever have to use the skills you learn there (I hope not), but you'll feel more secure. Plus, CPR skills last a lifetime and you may be able to help someone else's baby in an emergency someday.

Tell your partner the dreams you have about your child, and your worries about being a good dad. Open communication about your dreams and concerns can give each of you comfort and confidence.

Crib Notes _____

Don't think something's wrong if your reactions don't follow this schedule. You're liable to experience any of these thoughts and feelings any day that you're expecting. Just remember that all of these responses are natural and help prepare you to be a great dad.

Month Seven

Her: She's feeling fetal movement regularly, maybe even on a daily schedule that indicates when the baby is awake and asleep. Some moments she may feel complete satisfaction and confidence about this pregnancy and motherhood. Other moments she may be deeply anxious about whether she or the baby will develop problems, or whether she can be a good mother.

She may now occasionally get a so-called "false" contraction. At first, they may not even hurt. These Braxton Hicks contractions (the medical term) briefly tighten the muscles around the uterus. "Don't worry, they won't start pushing the baby out," says Joy Dorscher, M.D. "In fact, these contractions are 'practice runs' that help the mother get ready for the real thing." Your partner's other physical discomforts continue. Fortunately, nature helps her forget them after delivery.

You: By this time, you've probably heard the fetal heartbeat, felt some kicks, and seen an ultrasound picture. These are very exciting experiences, and no one will blame you for proudly talking about them and showing off the ultrasound at work.

As delivery day draws closer, you may start worrying or even obsessing about your partner's health. Don't feel awkward if you're thinking more about the bad things that might happen to her in childbirth than you are about the baby's health—right now, she's more real to you. Remember that childbirth has never been safer than it is in our culture, and rely on the wisdom of other fathers on this one.

What you can do: By this point, you should be consistent and conscientious about childbirth education classes and "homework." If your partner needs to do stretching and strengthening exercises, do them with her. Same with breathing and other labor prep routines. Doing it together now can be fun, and make your actual labor day smoother.

Pregnant Pauses

My favorite part of the pregnancy was rubbing her tummy, feeling the hits and kicks when the baby was active. I know it sounds bad, but I *loved* parading my pregnant wife around because I really thought she was the most beautiful lady and epitomized the essence of womanhood.

—Andy

Month Eight

Her: The growing uterus is crowding her other organs like someone with a huge backpack on a subway car at rush hour. She has to concentrate a bit more on breathing, since her lungs are getting squeezed. Not to worry, the baby still gets plenty of oxygen—remember that nature has been at this birthing thing for a long time.

Her center of gravity has now shifted from her fanny (normal for everyone) to her abdomen and breasts. She'll feel (and often be) less graceful, and has to figure out new habits for doing simple things, because so much baby is in the way. It's easier for her to lose her balance.

She may have big time aches in her back, pelvis, legs, and feet. She's coming down the home stretch with a heavy load, so resting is almost always in order. Emotionally, it may still be a roller coaster of anticipation and agitation as the birth day—and the challenge of mothering—speed closer.

You: You might feel a little crazy and frantic now as you try to wrap up loose ends at work and home in preparation for the big day. Plus, the extra strain on your partner's body may keep feeding anxiety over her health.

As childbirth classes conclude and the ride to the hospital approaches, you may worry that you'll be a worthless puddle when she goes into labor and starts screaming in pain. However, your coaching classes have given you tools to cope, and there will be people there to help you do the job well.

What you can do: Prioritize when getting errands, chores, and work tasks done. Asking "Does this really need to be done now—or at all?" is good practice for the next few years, when such juggling is a daily affair. One of your priorities should be doing the laundry, since she's tired and may not have a ton of stamina. (It's easy; just read the detergent bottle.)

Keep massaging your partner and cheering her on. There may be days when you're downright giddy—run with that feeling! Lean on other fathers and sharpen your childbirth tools to help ease your labor and delivery anxiety. You probably have what it takes to be the most important helper for your partner, and be there to witness the miracle of your child's birth.

Month Nine (and Ten)

Her: She's as huge as she's going to get and most of the physical discomforts remain. Once the baby "drops" (shifts down into the pelvic area in the days/weeks before birth), some struggles—like difficulty breathing—may ease, but she's liable to feel slightly different stresses on her back and legs. The baby has run out of room to move around in there, so she's feeling more squirming and less kicking.

As the labor approaches, some women get quite calm, some get a bit more anxious, some become very excited, some are downright impatient, and others swing around through a number of moods. Often she'll break out into an energetic rush of cleaning and organizing the home—that's called the nesting instinct. It's a very handy and nice thing.

You: You may be in "nesting" mode, too, animated by a desire to make everything just right for the baby's arrival. Encourage the excitement and the energy bursts that "nesting" brings. You both are going to need that energy during labor (and for years afterward). Your impatience for an end to expecting may be growing, too.

Things may feel simultaneously more real and more mysterious for you in the waning days of pregnancy. Remember that those feelings are not contradictory—a new baby is real and a mystery, which is what makes him so wonderful and fun.

What you can do: Be patient and encourage patience. Especially if you pass your due date, remind yourself and your partner that the due date is an estimate, and it won't be much longer. Don't ridicule her nesting behaviors. Instead, join in the spirit to stimulate your own nesting contributions, which lay solid foundations for bonding with the baby once she comes.

Keep on massaging and keep on cheering. And keep your bag packed for the hospital.

You Have Needs, Too

Don't forget that expecting is stressful for Mom and Dad both. When we're stressed, we men often put on what educator Jackson Katz calls our "tough guise." We think we can't ask for help or let any vulnerability show.

The antidote for stress is to actively and consciously care for your body and your spirit.

Pregnant Pauses

Most veteran dads say that they regularly need help and guidance with their fathering—and that things go best when they ask for it. They also say that being "vulnerable" is one of the greatest challenges and joys of fathering. You may think vulnerability is a weakness. For fathers, it's the open door through which we bond with our children, giving us the *strongest* human connections we may ever have.

Feeding Your Spirits

The first step in keeping your spirits up is to communicate, communicate, communicate (have I mentioned that before?) with your partner, family, friends, and the health-care pros. Let them know what you need, what you're thinking, and what you're feeling. Yes, even what you're feeling!

Open communication releases the pressure valves and makes it easier to tune into the good, exciting, energizing things happening in your pregnancy. Regular doses of exhilaration will give you energy and adrenaline to carry you through the stresses of expecting—and even labor and delivery!

Feeding Your Body

You have just as much incentive to take care of your body as your partner does. The better health you're in, the more stamina and resources you give your partner during pregnancy, as well as your partner and your kids for the rest of your life.

Be sure to exercise. You may not get to the gym or play softball as often as you did before you were expecting, but don't drop out completely. Exercise definitely helps reduce stress and anxiety, which are frequent visitors over these nine months. Plus, they help you stay in touch with your body.

It may seem paradoxical, but staying attuned to your body can deepen your connection to the pregnancy. Pregnancy forces your partner to be very conscious of how her body is working. If you do the same with your body, then it helps you be in a sharing, empathetic frame of mind with her.

Another must is eating well. If you haven't already, starting to eat a balanced and healthy diet (and forgoing toxic chemicals like nicotine) will give you the energy and clear-headedness to be ever more useful to your partner and kids.

If your partner has to observe special nutritional guidelines during pregnancy, you should follow them, too. Only a saintly woman doesn't resent it when her partner pigs out on a cheese steak and banana split across the table from her salad and fruit. So don't be rude at mealtime and leave a bad taste in her mouth. Go along with her meal plan. If you absolutely must have a banana split, get it at a restaurant, by yourself.

Removing Resentment

Speaking of resentment, throw it out of your expectant dad's toolbox, and don't let it back in. You will be tempted at times to feel resentful—for example, when she gets all the attention and you seem to be ignored. But choosing resentment as a tool to respond is bound to jam your gears.

The reason is simple. Resentment eats away at the resentor long before it has much impact (if any) on the resentee. When you resent something that's happening, the first person you undermine is yourself. Plus, resentment never changes the problem. Change comes from action and constructive attitudes. If an expectant dad is resentful, then he can expect nothing but trouble. So don't go there.

The Least You Need to Know

- Many exciting things happen to a woman's body and emotions during pregnancy.
- Many similar things happen to your body and emotions.
- You are your partner's first and best resource for handling pregnancy's challenges and discomforts.
- Sex during pregnancy is usually okay.
- Taking care of yourself is crucial to successful pregnancy, childbirth, and fathering.

Chapter 5

Getting Your Home Ready

In This Chapter

- Making spaces for baby
- Your essential to-buy list
- Doing things safely
- Cooking and cleaning for dads

As you learned in the last chapter, a successful full-term pregnancy eventually produces an infant (duh!). You will have to take the baby home with you (double duh!).

The place that you live has to be made ready for that big day, and there are a lot of details involved. For example, if you've never had a baby before, it's hard to imagine all the things you'll need around the house to keep the baby warm, fed, safe ... and sleeping undisturbed. In this chapter, you learn what to have waiting when Junior comes home.

What You *Have* to Buy (Everything Else Is Optional)

I don't know how they do it, but every childbirth magazine and infant gadget manufacturer seems to get a sample or catalogue in your mailbox a week after your partner's positive pregnancy test. Often, they use a very hard sell; something like:

> Don't let your baby's brain be irreversibly stunted!!! Get the new Bert and Ernie combination rubber pants and CD player. Call now and we'll include a FREE CD of Bert reading the poetry of Emily Dickinson and Ernie singing the table of elements! Guaranteed to get your child potty trained and into Harvard, or your money back!

This may be your first time as an expectant dad, but you're not a sucker. Nevertheless, there are folks ready to make a quick buck by playing on your insecurity or inexperience. A little common sense is the best defense. The following sections list the essential things to buy (or borrow).

Car Seats

Even a stubborn "I didn't need a car seat, so why does my kid?" dad can't get very far without one. The hospital won't let the baby out the door unless you have an up-to-date child safety seat (the "official" name for car seats), properly installed in your car.

A car seat keeps your baby from flying around inside the car during a crash, and forms a protective barrier that absorbs the force of a crash. Never put a child in any kind of vehicle without a functioning, correctly installed child safety seat.

If you borrow one from a friend or family member, make absolutely sure that:

- It still meets the current government safety standards.
- It isn't broken or damaged in any way.
- You know the proper way to install and use it.

The National Highway Traffic Safety Administration regulates car seats, and has excellent, easy-to-use information about them at www.nhtsa.dot.gov/people/injury/childps/. Or you can call the NHTSA Auto Safety Hotline at 1-800-424-9393. (In Washington, D.C., call 202-366-0123.)

Crib Notes

Never put a child in any kind of vehicle if he isn't properly strapped into a functioning, correctly installed child safety seat. Period. It ain't worth the risk. Not even once.

Strollers

Even your manly arms will get tired if you try to carry your baby (and all her equipment) around

town. Strollers take a load off you, and their movement is both stimulating and soothing to the baby.

Whether you're buying or borrowing, safety comes
first. The Juvenile Products Manufacturers Association (JPMA) says that the stroller must have a base
wide enough to prevent tipping, even when your
baby leans over the side. If the seat reclines, the
stroller must not tip backward when she lies down.

The JPMA website (www.jpma.org) also gives
guidelines for safe *operation* of a stroller:

- Parents should always secure the baby by
  using the stroller seat belt.

- Never hang pocketbooks, knapsacks, or
  shopping bags over the handles—the stroller
  could tip.

- Always use the locking device to prevent
  accidental folding and apply the brakes to
  keep the stroller from rolling away.

- When parents fold or unfold the stroller,
  keep the baby's hands away from areas that
  could pinch tiny fingers.

Crib Notes

It makes little sense to get a heavy-
duty, protective stroller for jogging if you
are going to risk your child's life by running down a very busy road. So use your
head and stick to slow speed limit residen-
tial streets, or car-free paths.

A simple, fold-up "umbrella" stroller will cost less than $40, and the fanciest jogging strollers (the ones marathoners use—what are they thinking?) run more than $500. Think through your situation and needs before purchasing one.

Cribs

After enjoying regular doses of your baby's boundless energy, you will cherish the moments when she's asleep. That's why it's crucial to have a safe crib that promotes undisturbed rest.

The biggest crib issue is infant safety. The baby's head or limbs must not have anything to get caught in or tangled on. Whether the crib is new or used, the Consumer Products Safety Commission says to make sure that:

- It has adequate strength and stability in the frame and headboard, a secure fitting mattress support structure, and a label certifying that the crib complies with the Commission's standards for cribs.
- The slats are no *more* than 2⅜ inches apart (the distance required by law for all new cribs). Anything wider risks trapping a limb or head. Don't use a crib if *any* slats are broken or missing.
- All the hardware is present and in good condition.
- When the crib is assembled, all the pieces securely attach and the mattress fits snugly.

- All screws and bolts fit tightly and do not turn freely in the wood. If a screw cannot be securely tightened, replace it with a larger one that can. Also, check the wood joints to be sure they are not coming apart.
- The mattress support hangers secure firmly to the hooks on the posts.
- If you have doubts about the condition of your crib, have it repaired or discard it.

If you use an older crib, it may have corner posts that reach higher than the rail. Those posts can snag a baby's clothes and cause real trouble—even strangulation. If you don't want to saw off the posts, get another crib. If there's any chance that a hand-me-down crib has lead paint or doesn't meet safety standards, throw it away. It isn't safe for *any* baby to use.

Use a firm mattress that fits snugly in the crib, and then cover it with a fitted sheet that fits snugly over the mattress. You don't want any part of the baby getting tangled up in loose sheets, or caught between the mattress and the sides of the crib (snug = safe). Also, some research indicates that a firm mattress reduces the incidence of Sudden Infant Death Syndrome (SIDS).

Never put a pillow in an infant's crib. She doesn't need it, and it's a suffocation risk. The same is true with heavy blankets and comforters. If Grandma made the baby an elaborate quilt, hang it on the nursery wall. The baby needs small, lightweight blankets.

Diaper Depot

Most people call this a changing table, but I'm a fan of alliteration. Besides, "table" doesn't really describe all the different kinds of furniture (tables, dressers, chests) people buy, borrow, or adapt for baby-changing headquarters. Again the first priority is infant safety.

Make sure that there is *no* way that the baby can roll off the working surface. The working surface should have low sides and pad covering it. The pad should either be waterproof (we *are* talking diapers here) or have more than one waterproof cover, so you can replace when needed.

Crib Notes

If you have twins, or triplets, or more, you'll need multiples of baby gear, too. Be ready to borrow and to experience the kindness of strangers. When we had twins, people we hardly knew gave us gifts of clothes and supplies. Neighbors and friends stepped forward with offers of an extra crib, playpen, stroller, etc. My sister gave us two months of diaper service (bless, you Ellen!). Be open and gracious in accepting gifts (people usually give them with no strings attached), and don't be too proud to borrow.

The changing table must have all your supplies within very easy reach of one hand. That's because

you always want to keep the other hand on the baby!
You should be able to easily reach fresh diapers;
those moist, disposable, butt-cleaning things we
euphemistically call "wipes"; skin ointment; and
other materials. Sound like a juggling act? It's the
first of many!

Infant Seat and High Chair

You may not need an infant seat or high chair right
away, but you will soon. An infant seat has sides
and holds the baby halfway between upright and
totally reclined, and you can set it on the floor,
chair, or table (as long as it's a safe, stable location
and you always keep an eye on him). You use an
infant seat so that he can look at you, and you can
feed him solid food. He won't be eating solid food
for a while, but many babies like sitting in an infant
seat anyway.

A high chair allows you to sit the baby near or at
the eating table. You don't start using it until the
baby can sit up by himself, usually at six months or
older. It comes with a seat belt (as does an infant
seat) and a removable tray. As with everything else,
make absolutely sure that the seat is safe, meets current standards, and you know how to operate it properly. Don't ever put a high chair on an unstable or
uneven surface, let its screws or structure loosen, or
use it as a stepladder.

Preparing Your Home

Because you're not an idiot, you already know that
bringing a baby home from the hospital is not

quite the same as moving a new roommate into that old "singles" apartment where you stacked empty beer bottles in the window. And while you might have had a childish housemate in the past, adding an infant to your home is a lot more complicated.

Fortunately, preparing your home for the baby is an area where you can shine big time. If you have an ounce of organizational, woodworking, painting, or other "handyman" skills, you can have a lot of fun and be very useful.

Setting Up the Nursery

What constitutes your nursery (or "the baby's room") will depend a great deal on the size of the place you're living. It may be a two-room suite in a mansion, or a curtained corner of a small apartment living room. It doesn't really matter to the baby.

What matters is having a space that's always safe, and can be made quiet whenever he's asleep.

You've already heard about the nesting instincts expectant dads develop. Readying the nursery is a concrete way we express our need to build a nest. You may feel motivated to completely remodel a bedroom just for your new child. That can be a lot of fun.

There are four simple rules for getting the home ready to house and nurture your baby:

- Safety first. And second, and third, and …
- Don't bite off more than you can chew (once the baby arrives, there's no time to polish off a half-finished remodeling job).

- Do it together. Working with your partner on home prep can be fun, efficient, and creative. Really!

- Don't take yourself too damn seriously. Pink vs. paisley on the nursery wallpaper trim isn't worth a big argument with your partner. By the time your child notices your decorating choice, he'll be old enough to repaint the room!

If you paint or lay new carpet, do it early in the pregnancy, and keep your pregnant partner out of the room. New paint and new wall-to-wall carpet give off fumes which are unpleasant, and may be unhealthy for an infant. So allow enough time (in the case of carpet, this could be many weeks) for the fumes to leave the building. A fan continually blowing out the window really helps. If it's winter, don't install new carpet if you can avoid it.

Nursery Supplies

You need more than furniture to handle your baby. You also need some basic supplies:

- Diaper bag.
- Cloth diapers.
- Baby carrier.
- Feeding gear.
- Bath gear.

The Rest of the House

Child-proof your entire home *before* you have the baby. There's not much free time afterward, and before you turn around, she'll be a toddler exploring electric outlets with her fingers and crawling into every cabinet (she'll pick the one where you store the Clorox first).

You can get the materials you need at most hardware, department, and toy stores. If you like shopping online, Google "child safety kit" and you'll get sites that sell whole packages. As with anything about children, there are tons of products and alternatives out there. Use your head, and your knowledge of how your home is set up, when making these purchases. Also, many of these child-proofing tools will be in place for five years or more, so get ones that will last.

The absolute essentials are:

- Outlet covers for *every* outlet in your home.
- One or more safety gates.
- Cupboard/cabinet locks.
- Drawer latches.
- Grip tape or stickers for the floor of the bathtub (or sink, if you use it for bathing).
- A bath water thermometer.
- A baby thermometer.
- "Sponge" tape or other secure padding to cover sharp edges that an infant or crawling baby can bang into.

- A refrigerator magnet with emergency phone numbers and instructions for baby first aid, CPR, and choking.

In addition to buying things, you have to do things, too. Store all chemicals, household cleaners, medications, and other dangerous substances out of the reach of your child. Don't leave tools, tacks, nails, etc., lying on the floor—in other words, use your head. Arrange things as if he was already a toddler, because those days come fast, and your head will be clearer now.

Enlisting the Support of Family and Friends

You will need the help of family and friends in the weeks, months, and years ahead. Most of the time, they'll be happy to help. Still, you have to be both gracious and judicious in accepting the help.

At the same time, you need to be clear about when and how you want help. You and your partner are the primary parents, and you have to figure out how to raise this child (if for no other reason that that grandparents eventually go home!).

Welcome the wisdom and experience of your parents and other people who have raised kids. But don't let them dictate what you do. If you have to, say lovingly and firmly, "Mom and Dad, I want your help and support. But in the end, we're the ones who have to learn how to raise the baby, so you have to let us make those decisions for ourselves. I'd even like you to let us learn from our mistakes."

Cooking, Cleaning, and Laundering

Back when I was a kid, my sisters cooked and cleaned, while I mowed the lawn and emptied the garbage. Once my sister asked why I had chores that only needed doing one day a week, while she had to cook or wash clothes and dishes every day. My mom replied, "Joe will learn to clean and cook in the Army." Besides expressing a flatly sexist attitude, her words made no sense because she was militantly opposed to my entering the Army!

Well, my man, if you haven't learned to cook, clean, and launder, now is the time to start. You and your partner will have your hands full with a new baby, so you're much better off if both of you can handle the most essential tasks around the house (like preparing something to eat). Plus, one baby will generate at least twice as many dirty clothes as the two of you generate alone.

The expectant months are an ideal time to pick up and/or refine your home front skills. You have time to experiment with recipes and cooking methods that suit your style, schedule, and personality. You have time to learn which of your partner's delicates can't go in the dryer, and how to iron your own shirts (tip: switch to permanent press, because you won't want to iron when there's a chance to play with the baby—or sleep).

For goodness sake, don't get hung up in the notion that cooking and cleaning are beneath a man. Cooking, cleaning, burping, changing diapers, earning money, comforting tears—it's all parents' work. Only a fool divvies up those necessary tasks by arbitrary (and silly) concepts of gender roles. As if those guys on KP and latrine duty in the Army aren't manly?

> **Pregnant Pauses**
>
> Do half the work, all the time, 24 hours a day, 7 days a week, 52 weeks a year. You'll need to figure out with your wife what this means. For example, I hate doing laundry and she hates cleaning the bathroom and mopping floors. She does most of the laundry and I clean the bathroom and mop the floors. Change half the diapers. Give half the baths. Do half the feedings—if the baby isn't breast-feeding, of course. Do half the night time rocking chair/baby walking duty. Always be a parent, never be a baby-sitter.
> —Chris

The Least You Need to Know

- Never drive a child without a child safety seat.
- Express your nesting instinct, but be realistic about how much time you have before the baby comes.
- Only use cribs, strollers, and other equipment that meet your needs and the latest safety standards.
- Don't let old gender expectations or family history get in the way of doing your part and getting the support you need.

Chapter 6

Getting Your Life Ready

In This Chapter

- You can't flunk childbirth class
- Choosing your method
- Babies are legal
- Planning your future

It doesn't do much good to bust your butt getting your home remodeled if you're not doing the other necessary things to prepare for your baby's arrival. This chapter deals with items that you might not have thought about, or may (mistakenly) think you don't really have to think about.

If you're going to be a fully involved father, then you need to get started now. And there are plenty of things to nail down which don't require a hammer. They do, however, require your time and attention.

Coaching Class

Nowadays, most parents go to childbirth preparation classes which prepare Mom for labor and delivery, while preparing Dad to "coach" her through them. No matter what childbirth approach you two choose, the classes you take will probably emphasize two crucial points (if they're worth their salt):

- Childbirth is a natural process, not a disease to be cured.

- A father is his partner's most crucial resource in pregnancy, labor, and delivery.

Dads and Dollars

Nearly every hospital and birthing center offers these classes, and they often have sliding fee scales. There really isn't anything else worth more investment of your time and money than childbirth classes. So show up!!!

Make sure you know who is sponsoring the classes, that the instructor is certified, and that you know the dates, times, and location of each class. Here's a very brief summary of your choices.

Lamaze

More North American parents use the Lamaze method than any other approach to childbirth. There are more Lamaze classes taught than any other kind (don't ask which is the chicken and which is the egg; I don't know). Created by (surprise!) Dr. Ferdinand Lamaze of France in the 1950s, this method teaches relaxation, external focus, and breathing to help parents to achieve a so-called "natural" childbirth. Dr. Lamaze built on his observations of Russian women who used Pavlovian conditioning to control breathing and relaxation so they could give birth without anesthetics. (Yes, this is the same dog-trainer/psychologist Pavlov you studied in Psych 101.)

Pregnant Pauses

Any childbirth that produces a living child and mother is a natural childbirth. So don't let anyone tell you that you "failed" if you had a cesarean delivery or choose to have painkillers administered during labor. You and your partner, working with your OB/GYN, get to make the call—not your neighbors, family, self-help books, or childbirth instructors. As one doctor (also a mother) says, "If Mom and baby are well at the end of the day, that's 1,000 times more important than how we get there."

The father is central to the Lamaze method. Dad coaches and does breathing exercises with Mom during the pregnancy (for practice) and during labor and delivery. Lamaze classes teach you how to do this, and usually include films of a delivery and information on cesarean deliveries, epidurals, and the like.

Lamaze encourages the mother to move around during labor, focus on comfort (e.g., having you give massages). It stresses that childbirth is a natural process (so it should be treated that way), and that babies shouldn't be separated from their mothers at birth. You can learn more and find a nearby class at www.lamzae.org, the home of Lamaze International.

The Bradley Method

The Bradley Method emphasizes healthy nutrition and avoidance of alcohol, drugs, tobacco, and the like during pregnancy, as well as the importance of being an informed consumer of medical services and family products. Bradley tends to have more weeks of class, but also covers a wider range of topics.

Crib Notes

If you and/or your partner can't get to childbirth classes in person (for instance, she's confined to complete bed rest, or you live on a remote ranch), you can get materials on tape and in books. Lamaze International has a comprehensive virtual class on videotape. Call 1-800-368-4404.

Like Lamaze, Bradley relies on breathing and relaxation. But Bradley encourages the mother's focus to be internal, rather than external. Mom learns how to close her eyes and get in tune with what's happening inside her body, thereby helping the process to go smoothly, naturally, and with less pain (in theory). Of course, the expectant father is key to coaching the mother through this process and keeping her focused.

Bradley also wants parents in charge of the arrangements for labor and delivery, and in charge of what happens there—while also prepared for emergency interventions (like cesareans) if needed. The official title of the Bradley organization is The American Academy of Husband-Coached Childbirth, and you can learn more at www.bradleybirth.com or 1-800-422-4784.

Leboyer

French obstetrician Frederic Leboyer thought that the bright lights, noise, and activity of the "normal" hospital delivery room was too much of a shock for a baby emerging from the dark, muffled, warm, and liquid environment of the womb. So he experimented with making the birth rooms more womblike.

Some research says his theories have merit—that babies born into dark, quiet rooms are calmer and more alert. Leboyer methods include having the mother (and father) partially submerged in a warm tub (one designed for labor and delivery) for the birth, and placing the baby on Mom's abdomen or at her breast for some time before cutting the umbilical cord.

The idea is to reduce the shock and stress of birth for the baby. For some parents, it has the benefit of reducing their stress and discomfort, too. Some hospitals have installed birthing pools, but not all have the expertise to use them at maximum potential. Ask a lot of questions if you decide to go this route.

More Techniques and Classes

Other training techniques for labor and delivery also stress that childbirth is a natural phenomenon, and not a medical condition. They just have slightly different approaches to relieve pain and promote relaxation during the process.

Some professionals find that hypnosis helps a woman moderate or even eliminate labor pain while increasing a relaxed state of concentration. Certified hypnotherapist, Marie Mongan, pioneer of something called HypnoBirthing, says it teaches women to self-hypnotize and use slow breathing methods that move in concert with her contractions. The idea is "to actually relax their body to the point it can work the way it was designed to work," Mongan says.

The Alexander Technique is a method of movement and exercise to reduce body tension and pain stemming from any number of sources, including labor. Created by F. M. Alexander, a Shakespearean actor from Australia, it relies on studying and altering body movement. Of course, it's not something you can master on your way to the hospital; you have to learn and practice from the early days of pregnancy. As with everything else, Mom's chances of benefiting are far better if you do the exercises with her. You can learn more from the American Society for the

Alexander Technique at www.alexandertech.com/
misc/pregnant.html.

A number of other associations and organizations
offer classes and resources for expectant parents.
These include:

- The Association of Labor Assistants and
  Childbirth Educators—www.alace.org, or
  617-441-2500.

- Association of Christian Childbirth
  Professionals—www.christianbirth.org.

- Childbirth and Postpartum Professional
  Association—www.childbirthprofessional.
  com, or 1-888-MY-CAPPA.

- International Childbirth Education
  Association—www.icea.org or 612-854-8660.

- Birthing from Within—www.birthpower.com
  or (505) 254-4884.

Why Be the Birth Coach?

The quick answer to the question of why you should
be the birthing coach is because your partner needs
you. There are many other tangible and intangible
reasons, too.

By going to childbirth classes and learning your
coaching techniques, you (and your partner) will
feel and be more in control of the pregnancy, labor,
and delivery. Knowledge is power, as they say (who
is this "they" who spout off all the time, anyway?),
and the more you know, the more you can decide
what works for you during the whole birth process.

You'll be able to guide, encourage, and comfort your partner as you two go through a stressful and miraculous time together. During labor, nothing beats your hands massaging her limbs, your fingers placing an ice chip between her lips, or your loving voice telling her that she can do this.

Best of all, being the coach means you get to be there in person to witness perhaps the most amazing thing you will ever see: your own child entering the world. A nurse took several photographs as I held and looked at my newborn twins. In every shot, the look on my face defines the word *agog*. Nearly every father who talks about being at his child's birth describes it as an incredible high and a miraculous experience.

Expectant dads often overlook one other excellent reason to be a birth coach: connecting with other dads. At childbirth classes, you'll meet other men who are expecting (most for the first time) just like you. In a good childbirth class, you'll have at least one session that includes a presentation from a veteran father about what to expect.

While we were in labor, I felt comfortable chatting with other expectant fathers in the OB ward, updating each other on our partners' progress. I wouldn't have done that if I hadn't seen firsthand in Lamaze classes that other men were—and wanted to be—intimately involved in their pregnancies. Your life as a father will be more satisfying (and easier) if you keep talking to other dads after you leave the hospital. I think of it as carrying that Lamaze intensity into all the rest of my fatherhood.

Pregnant Pauses

If you don't want to be in the delivery room for the birth of your baby, make your feelings known well ahead of time.

Some expectant dads are afraid that they'll panic, be sick at the sight of blood, or just feel too overwhelmed. Before making this decision, give it good, hard consideration, and talk it over with other fathers. Few dads are comfortable around blood, but even fewer even notice it in the excitement of childbirth.

If, in the end, you decide to patrol the waiting room instead of the delivery room, be prepared for your partner to feel disappointed. Do not blame her or fight with her about those feelings. And don't blame yourself, either—you are not a failure if you don't see your child born; you can still bond with him and be there every other step of the way.

Legal Issues

This may be the last thing you're thinking about, but once your baby is born, his legal status changes. He becomes a person under the law, with certain rights and—already—certain responsibilities (for example, the law says he needs a birth certificate and social security number).

The legal status, rights, and obligations of you and your parenting partner change, too. But because you are adults, those rights and responsibilities are more complicated. This section touches very briefly on some major issues—if you have any questions or need for further information, *please* contact an attorney, financial advisor, or other specialist.

Financial Issues for Pregnancy and Childbirth

Most parents starting a family are young and not exactly rich. No matter what your financial status, it really helps to have a family budget. For example, a budget can help you manage the temptation to buy every baby gadget that comes down the pike.

Create a budget. List your take home pay (after taxes) and an honest, realistic list of your expenses. Then, add in your estimate of the new expenses (one-time and ongoing) associated with having a child. This is not an easy process, because it almost always involves deciding to "cut" something—say, eating out more than once or twice a month. The budget decisions we make (and the way we make them) say a lot about our values and what's important to us. Getting a draft budget down on paper will help keep you from flying blind financially, and help you prioritize things so the baby gets what he needs.

There are tax implications when you have a baby— the biggest one is that you get a deduction for each child. However, a father can't claim this deduction if he isn't married or isn't the primary adoptive parent.

If your child is a U.S. citizen, you need to get her a social security number (she's going to need one anyway for the rest of her life). You'll need it before you can claim the child tax deduction. When getting information for the birth certificate, the hospital should ask if you want to apply for the baby's Social Security number. You'll have to give the Social Security numbers for you and your partner. The government will assign your baby a number and mail her Social Security card directly to you.

In Canada, your baby just needs a provincial birth certificate. She doesn't get her federal social insurance number until she gets a job.

You also need to start thinking about saving for your child's education. The first day of college is a long time off, but it will also be a lot more expensive— probably more than $30,000 a year for a public college, and more than $65,000 a year for a private one. It's smart to set aside a set percentage of your income for this purpose. It's best to use a financial planner to decide what saving tools (CDs, savings bonds, mutual funds, etc.) will work best for your situation and goals.

Insurance

Line up health insurance as early as possible for you and your partner. Check with your employer about signing up for the insurance (if any) they offer. Your child needs health insurance, too, since there will be a lot of doctor's visits ahead. Even if he is insanely healthy, he'll need check-ups, vaccinations, and the like—and they all cost money.

Many insurance companies don't offer coverage for pregnancy until after a waiting period of 250 days. And, in many cases, pregnancy insurance that doesn't come through a group policy is very expensive, making it tough for people who are self-employed or who work for a small company.

It is shocking to realize how many other barriers there are when trying to get comprehensive health insurance. For example, many insurers unfairly refuse coverage to women and men with infertility problems. You need to give careful thought and attention to the costs and complications, given the crazed state of health insurance in the United States.

Equally important, you and your partner should have life and disability insurance so that your child can be cared for if you should die or become disabled. No one likes to think about dying, even though it's the one thing we all have in common. But when you have kids, plan for the possibility that you'll die before they're grown. Denial won't pay the bills; life insurance might.

Your Will

While on the subject of death, you should have a will. If you have one already, update it *now* to account for the fact that you're becoming a father. A will is simply a legal document that tells how to distribute your assets and care for your minor children after your death. If you don't have a will, some probate judge you never met will make all those decisions for you. Not smart and totally preventable.

You must also choose a guardian to care for your child if you aren't around, and put that information in your will. (If just one of you dies, the surviving parent usually takes the role of guardian.) A guardian must be an adult and willing to take on the task— so don't name someone until you've talked to them about it and they've agreed to do it. Most parents choose a relative who shares the parents' values and beliefs about child-rearing and—most important— will love, comfort, and nurture the kids.

You can find forms to make a simple will online, in books, or at the library. However, when children are involved, it pays to create your will with the help of an attorney. Estate and probate law (the area covering post-death decisions) varies from state to state, sometimes substantially. So ask around for references for a local lawyer.

Establishing Paternity

If you're married, and listed as "father" on the baby's birth certificate, the law presumes that you are the biological father. However, things are not so straightforward if the parents are not married.

If you are the unmarried biological father, you should put your name on the birth certificate. But you should also take additional steps to "establish paternity" (the legal term) and do it sooner rather than later (you can do it later, but that makes it unnecessarily complicated). If your relationship with the mother breaks up before or after your baby's birth, you will need established paternity to fully assert your rights and responsibilities regarding child support, visitation, custody, and other issues concerning your child.

You can establish paternity by signing a declaration of parentage form (often available from your county social services office) and by having a paternity test. This test requires a DNA sample from you and the newborn (usually a swab taken from inside the cheek) for analysis by a laboratory. You can have the test done locally or use labs you can find on the Internet. Only use a laboratory accredited by the American Association of Blood Banks.

Other Unmarried Issues

If you and your partner aren't married, you need to check right away to see if your health insurance carrier will cover the expenses related to the birth. Some insurance companies do, and others don't; the same holds true for publicly-subsidized health insurance. It depends on how the insurer defines terms like household, family, and spouse; you don't automatically get the same presumption of rights in regard to your family as a married couple. That may not be fair, but it is reality.

You should also alter any life insurance and your will to list your new child as a beneficiary. Establishing paternity will help your child should he ever have the misfortune of losing you. Also, you should make open and informed decisions with your partner about whether and how to demonstrate joint ownership of assets like cars, homes, bank accounts, phone and utility bills, etc.

Most important, be an involved and engaged father. If your relationship with your partner should ever end, you will have to work out many of the same issues that a divorcing married couple does. Courts look at who is and has been caring for a kid when deciding custody questions. A judge will want to know who is making the child's doctor's appointments, arranging her birthday parties, attending school conferences, and the like.

If you don't know details about your child's medical conditions, medications, allergies, schedule, friends, etc., a judge will view you as being somewhat indifferent to the child. In other words, there can be big legal implications later for how tuned in and engaged you are in your child's life now. Of course, the real reason to do and know this stuff about your kid is that it's good for you and your kid. And that's why society (including the courts) put so much weight on it.

Issues for Homosexual Partners

Gay fathers don't have many of the same legal protections as nongay fathers. A gay dad has a hard time getting insurance and other employment related benefits for his child if she isn't his biological child. Even in adoption, some states recognize only one adult in a gay couple as the adoptive parent, leaving the other parent without legal standing. In other states, both men can petition for a joint adoption.

Under the law, the "legally recognized" dad is the only one allowed to decide on the health, education, and well-being of the couple's children. If the "legally recognized" father dies or is incapacitated, his partner may not have the right to become the legal guardian for their child.

Without the legal presumption that both fathers are legal parents, it's crucial to have written agreements about what you want to happen with your child. Obviously, you need a clearly articulated will for the worst situations, but you also need documents that deal with everyday situations (e.g., giving your partner "permission" to make medical decisions for the baby if he's the one there in the emergency room).

A good resource is Lambda Legal, a national nonprofit that uses litigation, education, and public policy to gain legal and civil rights for lesbians, gay men, bisexuals, the transgendered, and people with HIV or AIDS. Call 212-809-8585 or visit www.lambdalegal.org. You can get help creating a new will at www.gaywill.com/questions.html.

The Birth Plan

Many expectant parents write up a birth plan. This is a document stating what you want and expect to happen during your pregnancy, labor, and delivery. You list your desires about using anesthesia, getting an episiotomy, using a fetal monitor, who you want in the labor and/or delivery room, and the like. Work on it with your OB/GYN, because it's really an agreement between you and him or her about your vision for the birth.

A birth plan gives you a role in planning, and helps you be explicit about your wishes with each other and with the doctor. Of course, there's no guarantee that a breech baby won't poke a big hole in your quiet, incense-laden plans. The first priority is always the safety and health of the baby and Mother.

However, a birth plan is worth the effort. It is especially helpful if you go into labor while your OB/GYN is out of town or off duty. You can give the birth plan to the OB/GYN who does attend you, and he or she will have a concrete guide to your approach. So make sure you deliver a complete copy to your OB/GYN and the hospital or birthing center—and ask them to attach it to your partner's medical record. Make sure you have a copy, too, and then bring it with you when your partner goes into labor. IParenting.com has a guide (including samples) for creating a birth plan at birthplan.com.

The Least You Need to Know

- Decide early what labor and delivery method you'll use, then attend all the childbirth classes.
- Get your financial house in order before the baby comes.
- Update your insurance, will, and other legal documents to reflect your new role as Father.
- Understand the legal and other implications of adopting or giving birth outside of marriage.
- A birth plan helps you, your partner, and your OB/GYN have a more satisfying labor and delivery.

Neonatology 101

In This Chapter

- Getting ready to father
- Practice through pregnancy
- Handling the hurdles

I never gave the word *neonatology* any thought before I was an expectant father. And I didn't even begin to understand it until our premature twins entered the neonatal intensive care unit (or NICU, as abbreviation-addicted medical pros call it).

Neonatology is the study of newly born children. While newborn days are only a tiny slice of a person's life, they are probably the most intense. That's what gives neonatologists and new parents so much to ponder, talk about, and try.

When it comes to being an effective father, the first few days, months, and years of a baby's life are where the rubber meets the road. This chapter will give you some information and tools to help you stay in the race.

Using the "Transition" Time to Bone Up on Fathering

As an expectant father you are living in a transition time. Once you learn that your partner is pregnant, you immediately cease to be "man, but not a father." But you aren't quite a "man and father" yet either.

Fortunately, nature fills this in-between time with plenty of things to get you started on the road to fathering. It starts with changes in the hormones that increase in an expectant dad during his partner's pregnancy. These hormones and concern for our partner and baby-to-be create *couvade syndrome*, the phenomenon where expectant fathers feel "sympathy pains." These can be physical, psychological, and/or emotional changes.

In addition, your transition from man to dad includes many new responsibilities (like updating your living and financial arrangements) and opportunities to learn (like childbirth classes and conversations with veteran fathers).

All these in-between, expectant father experiences prepare you for being a full-blown father to a full-blown infant (who will promptly grow up before you know it).

Pregnancy's a Great Mimic

Your partner is irritable. She's huge and achy, so nothing seems to make her comfortable. You massage every part of her body, to little avail. She can't help getting up in the middle of the night, and waking you up, too. She has to pee every hour, or more. Her eating and sleeping schedule gets completely out of whack.

Other times, your partner is energized, with sparkling eyes and glowing skin. The feeling that she can conquer the world is so contagious that you feel that way, too. The two of you find new ways of snuggling, giving each other a deeper level of affection and comfort than you ever thought possible. You discover new and exciting qualities in each other almost daily.

Now, stop and think about what an infant spends time doing:

- Being irritated, but with nothing more than a variation in crying to tell you why.
- Gurgling and giggling when she lays eyes on you.
- Peeing (and pooping) over and over and over.
- Responding instantly to the feel and smell of your skin and hair, relaxing every muscle in his body.
- Screaming for no apparent reason.
- Getting up in the middle of the night, every night.
- Learning something new every day, and showing it to you.
- Teaching you something new every day about her and you.
- Eating on a schedule that defies any order and logic.

- Expending twice as much energy as you, even though his body is a fraction the size of yours.
- Making you feel like the most wondrous, powerful, and awestruck man in the world—all at the same time.
- Sleeping. Waking up. Sleeping. Waking up.

Starting to see a pattern here? The ways in which your partner's pregnancy affects your life mimic the ways that your newborn baby will affect your life. It may seem hard to believe right now, when life seems more intense than it's ever been, but this is only a shadow of what will be.

The Practice Floor

When you realize how pregnancy mimics parenting a newborn, you might just panic, or you might want to throw up your hands and jump overboard. Take a deep breath. In fact, your days as an expectant father help get your parenting sea legs under you.

Your expectancy is perfect for practicing the skills and attitudes you'll need as a dad. Your partner's feelings and behavior give you plenty of opportunity to practice—as do your own feelings and behaviors.

Start your practice with patience. Sometimes your pregnant partner is annoying and you'll be frustrated by everything you try to calm her down. Your infant will have those days, too. You learn what works best with your partner—be supportive, and patiently ride out her rough times, because they always end eventually. Keep that in mind when the baby comes—you may do everything you can to comfort her, and it still seems like her crying will never stop, but it does eventually.

Pregnant Pauses

For me, the best thing about Lamaze class was learning to deep breathe—really! I went to the dentist while we were pregnant, and used the breathing to keep me relaxed while he drilled my tooth. I memorized a spot on his ceiling, and it worked. Then I decided to use the breathing when I got tense and when Susan was getting tense. It worked great there, too. It doesn't work every time that I want to calm the baby down, but it works a lot of the time.
—Pedro

Perhaps the most important thing to practice, however, is openness to the excitement and wonder of pregnancy and childbirth because there are even more miracles ahead in helping a newborn grow.

While you're expecting, you'll have moments (or even days) when you are struck with amazement that:

- You and your partner started this incredible chain of events.
- Your partner's body is holding and nurturing a new life.

- You will get to see—and help—your own child be born.
- You have a deep and growing bond with someone you haven't even met yet.

Cherish these moments of amazement, and stay with them. They recharge and re-enthuse you for the home stretch of expecting, as well as the difficult times when you and/or your partner aren't feeling your best.

Relishing these moments is excellent practice for living with a newborn. You'll see unbelievable growth and development in your infant (if you're paying the least bit of attention!). This really is a miracle. As her dad, you'll be in touch with the miracle of the baby's life in a way no one else can be.

Crib Notes

Mayo Clinic researchers find that new dads worry about the health of their babies nearly as obsessively as new mothers do. According to the researchers, 58 percent of new fathers admitted having some form of irrational fear or thoughts about their new sons or daughters.

There will be days when you can almost taste the mysterious, visceral bond that develops between father and child. Those are the times when you feel like the roles have been reversed, and it is your baby who is giving *you* new life.

Now, every day will not be this heavenly. There will be days you'll feel frustrated, disjointed, and disconnected from your baby—just as you do sometimes with your partner. But if you immerse yourself in the good days, you will have reserves of energy and hope to get you successfully through the bad days and back into the good ones.

Crib Notes

Don't compare your baby to another one. Your baby may move ahead in socialization (eye contact, jabbering) and fall temporarily behind in the physical realm (crawling). Think of it like this: She's concentrating on one area, and once she masters it, she'll go back to the others.

Look for the parallels between how you feel while you're expecting and how you expect you might feel when your daughter or son (or both) arrive.

The Least You Need to Know

- Your "transition" time as an expectant father is ideal for learning how to be an involved father after birth.
- Pregnancy mimics life with a newborn, so it's a good time to practice parenting skills.
- Be sure to bask in the miraculous nature of conceiving and having a baby.

Chapter 8

A Labor Day Birthday

In This Chapter

- Getting to the hospital
- Making it through the day
- Labor stages
- Getting through to the doctor

A lot of things happen during labor and delivery, including some you can't anticipate ahead of time. Your job: Keep your focus centered on your partner, and then on her and the baby. Luckily, you have many months to line up the logistics that make smoother sailing for your partner, your baby, and you.

This chapter tells you how to get ready for the trip to the hospital and what to do when you get there. Fortunately, between birthing classes and the tips you'll get here, you can be at your best with all your resources lined up and ready to use.

Logistics Commander

When you and your partner decide it's time to go to the hospital, you will be operating on adrenaline, euphoria, and panic. Do your clear thinking *ahead* of time. Then, when you're called into action, you can just grab your gear and run.

Logistics Part 1: Transportation

By now, you know what hospital or birthing center you'll use for the birth. Make absolutely sure you know how to get there! A couple months before the birth, try driving to the hospital at different times of the day. This gives you a sense of the traffic flow, how much time to allow at rush hour vs. 2 A.M., and ideas for alternate routes if an accident stops traffic.

At home, make sure the phone number for your OB/GYN and the hospital are prominently displayed, so you won't forget where they are under pressure. From month eight on, make sure you keep your gas tank full, battery charged, and the car otherwise ready to go. Install the child safety seat in the back seat, so you don't have to remember it after the baby is born. And make sure you know where to find a set of car keys.

Recruit someone who lives nearby as a backup driver. A woman in labor *should not drive!* Make sure your backup has a car (or can easily access and drive yours) and will be available when you're not. Don't pick someone who works the same shift you do or who lives too far away.

Crib Notes

Don't tear the house apart looking for the car keys when labor comes. Make at least three extra keys now. Put one inside your wallet and one in your partner's purse. Hang one by the door you use to leave the house and get in the car. If you have a back-up driver, make sure he or she has a key, too.

If you plan to use public transportation, travel the route weeks ahead of time. Do it at different times of day, so you get a sense of how long it will take. Have a backup plan in case your partner goes into labor at night after the busses stop running. Treat your bus fare the same way drivers treat their car keys. Put an envelope by your front door with exact change or a fare card for the subway, and/or enough cash to pay a cabby.

If you don't have a car, a taxi is your best option. Call the cab company a few weeks before your due date and find out how fast they can get to you at different times of day, and whether it'll take longer on a weekend. If, when the time comes, none of these options will work, call an ambulance.

Logistics Part 2: Supplies

You will be at the hospital for hours and maybe days. The hospital has the basic tools for labor and delivery, but not other things you may want or need.

Get a good size bag or mid-size suitcase, fill it up with gear, and have it ready by the door you'll run through on your way to the hospital. The bag should include materials for your partner, the baby, and even for you!

I've adapted the following three lists from ones created by the Cleveland Clinic, and added a few practical suggestions. Don't go overboard—you'll want to fit everything in one bag that you can easily carry with one hand, because your first priority is keeping track of your partner (and you may be schlepping the bag all over the hospital).

For your partner, start with the following, then ask her what else she wants to bring—keeping comfort as priority one.

- Personal toiletries—toothbrush, toothpaste, hair, and skin-care items.
- Eyeglasses or contacts and supplies. Bring an extra pair just in case.
- Night gowns for one or two nights (hospital gowns are provided, but her own will probably feel better) and a robe.
- Slippers and warm socks.
- Cotton underwear (three or four pairs) and nursing bras.
- Heavy flow menstrual pads. There will be discharge after the birth and she'll want these.
- A list of names and phone numbers of people you'll want to call to share your news.

- A book or magazine to help pass the "hurry up and wait" time inevitable in many institutions.

- Comfortable clothes (and shoes) to go home in.

- Camera, camcorder, or tape recorder (with film, blank tapes, battery, and charger).

- Personal CD or tape player with one or two albums to soothe her, and one or two to energize her.

- A focal point. Some childbirth classes encourage Mom to focus on an external object while breathing through labor. We brought a big stuffed orange Pooh bear. My wife ended up not using him, but I hugged Pooh when the stress got high!

Dads and Dollars

Don't bring valuable jewelry, credit cards, or large amounts of cash to the hospital. Hospitals can be a bit chaotic, so don't bring fragile items either. If your partner wants some comforting reminder of home, bring a teddy bear, not a precious porcelain knickknack.

The hospital will have the baby supplies you need for the first few days, like diapers. Many hospitals send you home with a goodie bag of free baby products donated by manufacturers to win your brand loyalty. But your new baby still needs some items from home.

You can lean down to your partner's belly and ask what your baby wants, but you won't get an answer. You'll have to choose (don't bring him candy bars yet, okay?). Here's where to start:

- Undershirts.

- Socks (don't bring shoes—a baby shouldn't wear shoes until she can walk; they're bad for her feet).

- Receiving blankets—at least three. (I don't think you get a shipping blanket until you ship the kid off to camp.)

- Clothes to go home in. A simple "sleeper" outfit is best. Include a hat, even if the weather is warm. If it's cold, bring a baby sweater or snowsuit.

- Infant car seat. Remember, they won't let you take the baby home without one. Don't try and fit this in the bag! (Leave it in the car until you need it.) Make absolutely sure that the seat is properly installed. Many car accidents that kill children are a result of improperly installed car seats.

Supplying the Supplier

In war movies, tanks and planes roar endlessly into action. They never make movies about the people who put the gas and ammo into the tanks. However, any strategic commander will tell you that the side with better logistical support usually wins.

Dads and Dollars

Many hospitals don't allow cell phones because they may interfere with equipment. Check with your facility; if you can't have one, make sure you have coins for local pay phone calls and a phone card for long distance. If you can have a cell phone, you'll use it a lot, so bring the charger.

While you're filling the bag with things for your partner and baby, keep room for the things *you* will need, too, which should include the following:

- Personal toiletries. Even if you don't spend the night in the hospital, you may want to brush your teeth.

- Your medications. You don't want to pass our during labor because your insulin is at home in the bathroom.

- Clothes to sleep in. If you stay over, hospital rooms are not as private as bedrooms; wear a sweat suit or something similar for sleeping.

- A change of clothes (including underwear and socks).

- Snacks like granola, dried fruit, nuts, and maybe even a Milky Way Midnight bar. Your partner can't eat during labor, but your energy level must remain high. Plus, the morning after the birth, she may be more ravenous than the hospital kitchen can handle.

- In *The Expectant Father*, Armin Brott wisely suggests bringing a bathing suit, especially if you're using a birthing tub or the hospital lets Mom take a shower to relax during labor. A swimsuit lets you join her without scandalizing the staff.

- A form for the baby to sign, legally obligating her to support you in your retirement. (Just kidding.)

If you do bring any extras, keep it simple and keep it in one bag. There are a lot more important things to keep track of than CDs and socks. And don't even think about going shopping while she's in labor.

Crib Notes

> Bring only "low-odor" food to the hospital. During labor, your partner may be hypersensitive to smells and gag if she finds garlic on your breath as you whisper encouragement in her ear. Stick to simple, high-energy foods that won't smell in the bag or in your mouth.

In the end, the hospital will have everything you really need for a successful birth—the mother, you, and the baby. Everything else is optional. If she goes into labor at your parents' house, don't go home for your supply bag—get her to the hospital!

When Do We Go to the Hospital?

As the expectant months wind down, this is the most pressing question for most couples. Believe it or not, most first-time parents know when to go. How can they know if they're rookies? Nature has her ways.

You and your partner should be well tuned in to each other by now—if you're doing what this book says! You can pick up on cues from your partner, some tangible and others intangible, which indicate that this is the real deal, even if she isn't so sure.

My wife's cervix started dilating a month before her due date, so the doctor ordered complete bed rest (for her, not me). One morning a week later, she said she thought maybe her water had broken, but that she didn't think we needed to go to the hospital because she didn't feel any strong contractions.

OB/GYN

Even if you get to the hospital "too soon" and they send you home, don't get frustrated or embarrassed. View it as a practice run and remember: going early is better than waiting too long. Then, stay tuned, because your labor day is coming soon one way or another.

I said, "Are you crazy? I think we should go right away if your water broke." She said no, I said yes; we played verbal tennis for a few minutes, as couples do. Finally, I insisted on at least calling the hospital and explaining the situation. The nurse said, "Are you crazy? Get in here right away if her water broke." Our twins were born by 7:30 that night.

"False" Labor

Starting as early as week 20 of her pregnancy, your partner may feel Braxton Hicks contractions, named for British gynecologist John Braxton Hicks, who first described them in medical literature back in 1872. Some people say Dr. Hicks *discovered* this type of contraction. But as Janine DeBaise writes ironically in the spring 1996 issue of *Midwifery Today*, "This was sort of like Columbus discovering America. Some people already knew it was there."

Braxton Hicks contractions are like wind sprints for your partner's uterus, warming up its muscles for labor contractions and softening up the cervix.

The American Pregnancy Association describes them as:

- Irregular in intensity
- Infrequent
- Unpredictable
- Nonrhythmic
- More uncomfortable than painful
- Not increasing in intensity or frequency during an episode
- They taper off and then disappear altogether

They last from 30 seconds to 2 minutes, and can be stimulated by dehydration or exercise. Your partner can usually ease any discomfort by taking a warm bath, changing her body position (rest if she's moving, move if she's resting), drinking water, or practicing her breathing. By the way, Braxton Hicks contractions don't hurt the baby at all.

Be especially vigilant if she is a high risk for delivering prematurely. Call the OB/GYN right away if contractions come more than four times in an hour, produce bloody or watery vaginal discharge, generate lower back pain, or develop a regular pattern. These symptoms may mean labor is starting, and you need to respond right away.

Early Labor

Labor has what doctors call three "stages" and the first phase has three "phases." Why they don't just make it five stages, I don't know. But you go to the hospital near the end of stage one, phase one, so let's take a look at it.

Usually, stage one, phase one is the longest part of labor, sometimes known as early or latent labor. It is normally the least painful and can actually start days or weeks before the birth day, in which case your partner may not notice it much. It can also come on suddenly with contractions she can't miss, and then last anywhere from 2 to 24 hours.

Her contractions will be what doctors call "mild to moderate" and they generally last less than a minute each. While they may grow more frequent, they haven't yet developed a regular pattern.

OB/GYN

Stage One of labor has three phases, based on the dilation of the cervix:

- **Phase one:** Relatively mild contractions start dilating the cervix to 3 centimeters (out of 10).
- **Phase two:** Cervix dilates up to 7 centimeters, as contractions intensify.
- **Phase three:** The cervix dilates completely to 10 centimeters, beginning the transition to delivery.

Stage Two consists of delivering the baby.

Stage Three consists of delivering the placenta.

In a low-risk pregnancy, most OB/GYNs recommend waiting until the end of phase one or the start of phase two before going to the hospital. So your job during phase one is to keep your partner comfortable, relaxed, and rested. Her toughest challenges are likely to be cramps and back pain. It's normal for her to have a mucousy vaginal discharge laced with blood, as well as diarrhea and/or indigestion.

Do everything you can to smooth the transition to phase two. Rub her back and help her move into positions that feel better. Try sitting on the floor up against a wall, and have her sit between your legs as you hold her body almost upright; this relaxes her, and provides the comfort of your embrace. Do breathing exercises together to help her through the discomfort.

Encourage her to do what feels good, even if it looks silly. Some women find relief by standing and leaning their heads against the wall. Some get down on hands and knees to get the pressure off their spine. These are examples of my daughter's old adage: "Gravity is our friend."

If she's hungry, give her light, easy-to-digest foods and fluids. Don't go for a fast-food burger or ice cream; stick to mild soup and toast, which won't make her sick later. If phase one begins during the day, work to "normalize" what you do. Distract her with a walk, a TV show, or by cooking a meal or folding the laundry together.

Keep a sense of humor and a calm, confident attitude. It's a lot easier to chuckle now than later. Keep the tone light and laugh at the absurdity of making a casserole to freeze when you're only hours away from having a baby.

OB/GYN

Conventional wisdom says regular intervals of 5 or 10 minutes between contractions signal the start of active (phase two) labor. However, some women never have a consistent, timed rhythm to their intervals. If contractions are longer, stronger, and more frequent than before, call your doctor and/or go to the hospital. If you get there "too early," you won't be the first or last parents to do so, and the nurses won't laugh at you.

Keep yourselves rested, because you both need every ounce of reserves later on. Getting all wound up now won't help later. If it's nighttime and you haven't reached phase two, help her get to sleep and stay asleep. Then, you go to sleep, too.

Take charge of remembering details of the contractions. Time the interval between the start of one and the start of the next one. When they get to be fewer than 10 minutes apart, you're closing in on phase two and your trip to the hospital.

If you have any doubt about whether it's time to go to the hospital, call your OB/GYN or hospital. If your partner's water breaks, head there right away.

Hit the Road, Jack

By the time you've reached stage one, phase two, you should be at the hospital. Phase two is often called "active labor" because contractions last longer than earlier ones and are markedly more intense. As one doctor says, "If a woman calls me on the phone during a contraction, I can usually tell by the tone of her voice whether she's ready to go to the hospital."

At the Hospital

When taking your partner to the hospital, your first task is to do it calmly and safely. Call ahead before you leave, if you can. When you arrive, make sure *you* fill out the registration and permission forms and field the questions (preregister when you first choose the facility to save time). Don't let any red tape waylay you from your first responsibility: being with your partner.

Someone will take you to your labor or birthing room, with a possible stop along the way in an assessment (or "triage") room. Staff will do diagnostic tests on your partner: blood pressure, pulse, urine sample, respiration, taking her temperature, checking her vaginal discharge, etc. They may set up a fetal monitor and require your partner to change into a hospital gown. Soon after arriving, she will have a vaginal exam, where the OB/GYN checks for cervical dilation and other progress.

If you have a birthing plan, make sure there's a copy in her medical record, signed by Mom *and* doctor, along with reasons why and when the plan can't be followed (e.g., fetal distress). Have a copy in the room with you to show to the staff and OB/GYNs, especially if your personal OB/GYN is not available. If the nursing shift changes, have the incoming staff read the plan—make sure your preferences are understood.

Make the room as comfortable as possible for your partner and you. Some women want the lights dimmed, mood music, and the door closed to block out distractions. Others want the distraction of hearing what's happening in the hallway, watching TV, and peppy music. Follow her lead, even when her direction does a quick 180.

Phase Two

In phase two, there's less time between contractions, so your partner has to concentrate harder on relaxing. She may get annoyed, impatient, and weary about this. Your number one job is to help her through it any way you can.

Because contractions are now longer and more painful, she is turning her attention completely to her body and what's happening to it. She'll have more of the vaginal discharge known as "bloody show," along with aching legs, growing fatigue, and backache.

Pregnant Pauses

When someone is hurting, it's natural to say, "I know how you feel." Erase that phrase from your memory bank during labor. If you say it, your partner may angrily remind you, "No you don't! You're a man and, damn it, you'll *never* know how this feels!" It's not worth her aggravation or your hurt feelings.

Some contractions are so intense that she can't even speak during them. She may despair that labor will ever end, and 30 seconds later feel elated that labor is progressing so fast. One moment she may cry desperately for your help, and the next she may gruffly inform you that she can do it all by herself. Go with the flow.

Pain relief, like an epidural, has to be given before the end of phase two (if you and your partner decide to go that route). Ask your OB/GYN when the "deadline" is—the time after which it's too close to delivery for him to administer pain medication.

Phase Three

This last phase of stage one is the transition into stage two: delivering the baby. It can be the shortest phase, but also the toughest, because your partner has been at this for a while now, and wants to get it over with.

Fighting the impulse to "get this over with now!" may be the biggest challenge of phase three. As her cervix reaches full dilation, she will have the seemingly irresistible urge to push the baby out. You must help her hold back until the OB/GYN says it's time to start delivery.

You may have heard stories of women in labor telling their partners, "I am completely fed up with this and I'm going home," or, "How did you get me into this? I'm never letting you touch me again!" These stories are true. It's normal for your partner to feel (and even say) these things.

Of course she can't go home and she will sleep with you again. But these feelings and thoughts stem from the pain, fatigue, fear, confusion, and frustration she's experiencing. It's a lot for her to handle. That means it's a lot for you to handle, too.

Your Labor Day Labors

You are your partner's key ally during labor and delivery. Now that the big day has arrived, you must pull out all that you've learned, combine it with the instincts nature gives you, and go the distance. This section gives concrete suggestions for what to do.

Aping the Rhino (or Don't Take It Personally When She Screams)

A friend says that he felt like an ape and a rhino during his wife's labor. "I acted like an ape, bouncing around being silly to distract her. And I needed the skin of a rhino to keep from being crushed by all the things she said to me. I knew she didn't really mean them, but they were hard to hear."

> **Crib Notes**
>
> Don't rise to the bait if your partner says things that would hurt your feelings if spoken at the dinner table. She's in pain and turmoil, so there's no point in discussing it—and it's beside the point, which is delivering the baby.

No matter what happens during labor, you need to present your partner with an upbeat, comforting, encouraging face. Labor isn't a time to work out long-standing issues in your relationship, even if she chooses this moment to throw them in that happy face of yours. Remember that it takes two people to have an argument. If you don't participate, she'll eventually move on to her next contraction or distraction.

What to Do in Phase Two

Now that she's in the hospital and encountering intense pain, you are her guide and companion. Help her relax and conserve energy between each contraction. Breathe along through each contraction, if she wants you to. It might make her tense or keep her from concentrating. But always remember that she can quickly change her mind, and stand ready to respond.

Acknowledge her pain. Don't say, "I know how you feel." Instead, say, "I know it hurts, honey, and I know you can make it through. You're doing great." Remember that she hurts even if she doesn't say anything; tell her that she doesn't have to be stoic for you.

Handle only one contraction at a time. Don't worry about the next one in the middle of this one. Don't criticize her or how she's doing things. Act the way you would want her to act if she was helping you through hours of intense pain. Encourage and reassure her. If encouraging words make her tense, then do it silently with your eyes and touch.

Work with her to make her comfortable. If the hospital allows her to take a walk or a shower, and she thinks it'll help, go with her.

Massage, massage, massage. She may like you to rub her feet all the way through labor, or she may make you switch spots every five minutes. Do what she wants. Some doctors say that massaging her back while she's sitting up may speed labor along. But if massaging makes her tense, use words to relax and encourage her instead.

Be her ice chip man. Many hospitals encourage women to suck on ice chips or frozen juice pops during labor. It's distracting and keeps her hydrated. Have the ice chips ready at all times and put them lovingly in her mouth whenever she wants them. At her other end, make sure she has warm socks if her feet are cold.

She may also like a cool washcloth on her forehead or other parts of her body. Keep them fresh as long as she wants them. Make sure to wring the cloth out thoroughly; dripping wet skin will annoy her.

Back off if your efforts annoy her. Her annoyance may pass quickly, or it may last hours. Either way, she *still* needs you by her side, ready to do what she wants to get through this.

Advocate and mediate for her with the hospital staff (more on this later). Make sure you understand any hospital suggestion before you okay it. Tell the staff if your partner wants medication to block the labor pains, but recognize (and help her understand) that many OB/GYNs will wait a half hour or so before giving the medications, in case phase three is about to start. We'll discuss pain relief options more thoroughly in Chapter 9.

What to Do in Phase Three

Phase three is the transition into the delivery stage, and your partner needs you to do more of what you've been doing. Remember that you are close to the goal line, so remind her how well she's passing all the yard markers.

As contractions get stronger and closer together, she may feel an irresistible urge to push. You must help her to resist until the OB/GYN says it's time. If the urge is overwhelming, and no one has examined her for a while, call a nurse and get the doctor in.

Be short and sweet in your words. Her concentration may be as intense as her contractions, so keep your coaching instructions simple and specific. She may be particularly sensitive to anyone touching her, so look for her cues.

Pregnant Pauses

For me, the baby just wasn't real. No matter how many times I heard the heartbeat, felt it move, watched my wife's belly jump with fetal hiccups, it just never came home. Not like it did the day I held my precious daughter in my arms and saw her with my own eyes. Tears were pouring down my face while I said, "Look, look, she's real! She's here." My wife just smiled and said, "I know. I've known for a long time."

—Dennis

She may be so caught up in the contractions that she can't keep track of them. Tell her when they start and stop, as well as their frequency. Hang in there! Delivery is just around the corner, and your instructions are just ahead in Chapter 9.

Don't Be Treated Like a Fifth Wheel

Health-care workers have more experience delivering babies than you do. Sometimes they treat an expectant dad as invisible or in the way. Hospitals are getting a lot better about this, but here are ways to prevent being treated like a fifth wheel, or address it if a "professional" rolls over you.

Simple and direct etiquette usually smoothes relations with physicians and other hospital staff. "When someone comes into your labor room, introduce yourself," Joy Dorscher, M.D., says. "It may seem repetitive if numerous people pass through, but say, 'Hello, I'm so-and-so, and I am the husband (or coach) here.' Most doctors and nurses want to know who you are, and be able to call you by name."

Most OB professionals welcome questions, and have experience explaining things in lay language. Ask (politely) why someone is doing a procedure, and ask if there is more than one option for you to consider.

"Be your partner's advocate, but not an obstructionist," Dorscher says. "Speak up, and don't be afraid to say, 'My partner is busy right now, can you explain to me what you're after, or why you're doing that right now?'"

The Least You Need to Know

- Labor is easier if you plan ahead for what to do and what to bring.

- Labor has three progressing stages. Stage one has three phases. Recognizing them helps you make good judgments.

- Medical staff should help you both, so be sure to stay included in discussions and decisions.

- You are a full partner in labor and delivery. Give the role everything you've got.

- Follow your partner's lead, and be her guide through labor.

- Keep a thick skin and remember that the mother and baby are more important than your pride.

Chapter 9

Delivery Day

In This Chapter

- Your labor choices
- It's a real pain
- The baby's here!
- Cesarean calling

Things move at a brisk pace after stage one of labor. But you probably won't notice. Many dads say that time slows down or becomes elastic once the OB/GYN says, "Push!"

I remember the surroundings of our delivery room in great detail, and remember many specific moments and movements—much more than normal for such a short span of time. The most vivid memory is seeing each of our children come out, actual people right from the start.

Even though events happen rapidly, you need to know what to do and when. This chapter guides you through this brief and miraculous moment in your life.

Make Way for Baby

If everything progresses the way it's supposed to, your partner's contractions have completely dilated her cervix, making an opening at the mouth of her uterus for the baby to slip through. The contractions also push the baby's head down to the cervix, and right on through into the miraculously expandable vagina, which now takes on its function of birth canal. (Why "canal" and not "tunnel?" Who knows?)

This is stage two of labor, delivery of the baby. Because delivery is messy and a bit bloody, some expectant dads fear that they will falter or faint, failing their partners right at the finish line. As my grandmother used to say (exaggerating her Bronx accent), "Yew shouldn't worry." In the heat of the moment, most every father is oblivious to the blood and commotion of a delivery room. Your gaze and attention zero in on your new baby and everything else falls away.

Pain or Not to Pain?

Labor hurts. That's the shortest, truest sentence you'll find in a book about pregnancy. It has hurt as long as women have given birth. Cultures older than ours (and, according to some, more "primitive") use herbs, prayers, rhythmic breathing, meditation, and other methods of diminishing the pain and/or distracting a mother from it.

In twenty-first-century North America, the most common ways to reduce pain during an unprob-lematic labor are:

- Breathing and relaxation techniques learned in birthing classes
- Pain-blocking drugs

After continuing commands (from your OB/GYN, birthing class, and this book) to avoid drugs during pregnancy, it may seem odd to have drugs routinely used on pregnancy's last day. You wouldn't be the only one to think it's odd. There is widespread, heated, often polarizing argument in the childbirth field over the use of medication during labor.

While my opinionated Irish genes tempt me to give the "final word" on this dispute, it's unlikely anyone would listen. Instead, I'll tell you briefly about the most common anesthetic techniques used in labor.

- **Epidural block.** The most common method, an epidural provides a pain-numbing drug that allows Mom to stay awake and alert during labor and delivery. Sometimes Mom gets an IV first, to minimize side effects. Then, she sits up while they put a needle (it looked huge to my untrained eye) in her lower back, injecting the drug into the epidural area of the mother's spine (hence the name). This procedure is short, but un-comfortable; you need to hold your partner close and perfectly still. It's usually done an hour or more before delivery, and can be used for some C-sections.

- **Spinal and Pudendal blocks.** These are given right before delivery. A spinal involves injecting a pain numbing drug into the lower spinal cord. Spinals have longer-lasting side effects than epidurals. In a Pudendal block, the doctor injects a pain killer into the vagina or perineum, usually before a forceps- or suction-aided delivery.

- **General anesthesia.** This is what doctors use to "put you under" during major surgery. In childbirth, it's used for emergency cesarean deliveries, and very rarely for vaginal births—although it was the standard method for years. Our mothers were out cold when many of us were born.

As with every other major childbirth decision, discuss the pros and cons with each other and your OB/GYN well ahead of time. But be flexible enough to respond to situations that arise when labor actually comes. If she's sure she wants drugs to numb the pain, don't argue with her (as if *that* would do any good); get the doctor.

If she is stuck in the early phase of stage one, the OB/GYN may recommend inducing labor. He'll also urge induction if the water has broken and contractions haven't started, haven't gotten into a regular pattern, or there are other reasons to move things along. Your partner will get an IV containing synthetic hormones to stimulate active labor. Induced labor may feel more painful for the Mom.

OB/GYN

Proponents of "natural" childbirth urge women to forego pain medication during labor. They argue that women gave birth without drugs for eons. That's true, but as fathering guru Armin Brott says, "They also died from childbirth in much larger numbers; and doctors used to do surgery without anesthesia or antibiotics. There's no one 'right' way to go through childbirth."

If you and your partner decide to skip medication, that's great. During labor, she makes the call (don't argue with her about it; it's her body). If she changes her mind, and opts for an epidural, that's great, too. Childbirth is "right" when Mom and baby make it through. Don't believe *anyone* who says that you "failed" by using medications during labor. It's simply not true.

In addition, your OB/GYN might give your partner and/or your baby antibiotics to counteract bacteria in the vagina. Babies passing through an infected birth canal have a good chance of catching the infection, so a course of antibiotics is not unusual. If there's an active herpes virus, a C-section is the only choice.

Stage Two and What to Do

In stage two, you do more of what you've been doing: encouraging, comforting, advocating for her with the staff, and soaking up the whole experience.

Your partner may seem exhausted after all this labor and you may tire of trying to keep her energy up. But many expectant moms and dads get a sudden power burst from the recesses of their souls for this last big push. Once again, nature finds a way!

Once the OB/GYN says it's time to push, work closely with your partner to get her through each effort, just as you've been doing with contractions.

Stay totally in tune with her and her needs, while also following the lead and instructions of the professionals. This can be your toughest walk on the tightrope between advocacy and obstructionism, but if things are progressing smoothly, most dads find that everyone in the delivery room is on the same page.

Stay loose. Don't lock your knees or stay in one position too long; release physical tension. You'll save energy and be more aware that way.

Some women say they don't remember hearing doctor instructions, but do remember their partners saying what to do. You may literally be the conduit from professional to Mom at this stage.

Don't get distracted by who else is in the delivery room. Our kids were the first vaginal delivery of twins in more than a year at an inner city teaching hospital. There were 18 people in the delivery room to watch: neonatal nursing students, OB residents, med students, and so on. Having never given birth before, we thought this was normal.

A few months later, I coached a friend through the birth of her second child (I was freshly trained, after all!). She used a different, nonteaching hospital. We entered the delivery room with one nurse and one doctor, so I waited for "the others" to arrive. When the doctor said, "The baby is crowning," I turned to the nurse and screeched, "Where is everybody?" The nurse replied, "We have everyone we need," with a strong implication that, since I was so clueless, they didn't need me at all. The baby turned out fine despite me.

Have I mentioned that there is no "normal" in pregnancy and childbirth?

> **Pregnant Pauses**
>
> When we had our second child, my 14-year-old stepdaughter was in the delivery room. Many thought we were crazy. However, I think two things: First, she has a deep bond with the baby after seeing the birth firsthand. And second, she told me afterward "I hope I have small babies." I think a little birth control was at work also.
>
> —Doug

It's a Baby!

In a "normal" birth, the baby's head is down and comes out first. The head is the heaviest part of the infant's body, so nature aligns it so gravity can lend a hand. It's a very tight squeeze to get that head through the cervical opening and birth canal, so the baby usually turns her head to fit. Nature also arranges things so that her skull isn't real hard, so the head can squish a bit to fit through. That's why some babies seem to have slightly "pointy" skulls when they're born. (It doesn't last.)

It's called "crowning" when the top of her head appears. But there can be a lot of time between crowning and actual birth, so it may feel like you're stalled (be patient). Eventually, things progress so that the person delivering either coaxes the rest of the head out, or just waits for it to drop into his or her hands. After the head comes through, Mom, baby, and delivery person conspire to wriggle the shoulders out. The remaining, narrower body parts easily follow the path that the head so considerately plowed. And, you have yourselves a baby.

You may have several options for what *you* do during the moment of birth. Be sure to talk about them with your partner and OB/GYN ahead of time, completing the necessary arrangements, and preparation.

Some facilities allow the father to actually deliver the baby, if there are no complications. You have to prep for this beforehand. The OB/GYN is right next to you all the time, just in case. This gives you the thrill of having your baby drop right into your hands as she leaves your partner's body. The one drawback is that you must (obviously) leave your partner's side to do this.

Pregnant Pauses

Seeing the baby's head appear in the birth canal was almost a supernatural thing. It was like I was at the scene of God blowing the breath of life into Adam's nostrils. Watching creation. It was indescribable really.

—Andy

You may choose to stand over the doctor's shoulder for a close-up look at the birth. This position also means leaving your partner's side. If you take still or video pictures from this angle, do not let the picture taking interfere with *experiencing* this fleeting moment. It is literally a once in a lifetime event; even if you have other children, you will never see this child born again.

Many hospitals now have delivery room mirrors that allow the mother to watch the baby emerge.

A few OB/GYNs and/or hospitals require the father to stay at the mother's head. Most places give you some leeway to move around the delivery room. But always remember that your first obligation is to your partner and helping her push the baby out.

Witnessing the delivery of your child can make your head spin. Remember to breathe! Periodic relaxation (deep breaths, a loud "aahhhh") helps you stay open to all that's happening, and makes you optimally useful to your partner and the baby. If you feel faint, sit down, and tell the nurse or OB/GYN how you feel. They may have a sugar source nearby to restore your equilibrium.

Cutting the Cord

The baby comes out of the womb with his umbilical cord still attached to the placenta. Doctors and midwives usually check things like lung ventilation and wait varying lengths of time (another source of childbirth debate) before cutting the cord.

Many fathers want to cut the cord themselves, and few doctors object, if the birth is smooth. In fact, many doctors now let dads cut the cord during a cesarean. But be ready, it's tough to cut through.

Fathering writer Mike Farrell says, "This is your rite of passage. Unless complications arise … take part in the cutting of the umbilical cord." It is an intimate, symbolic, and amazing experience for you. But if the thought of doing it makes you squeamish, don't worry. It's fine to let the doctor do it, and you'll still bond with the baby.

Stage Three

Remember stage three of labor? It doesn't get the attention of the other two stages, but delivering the placenta is necessary nonetheless. In another of nature's wonders, the placenta separates itself from the uterus wall when the child is born. Its job is done, and after the cord is cut, it needs to get out.

Fortunately, your partner's uterus still has contractions after birth, and those bring the placenta down to the cervix. However, she may still have to push the placenta out. In most cases, this is a simple matter, and it seems to happen almost incidentally; you two are absorbed in the new baby.

Outside North America, it's not uncommon for people to ritually show their gratitude for the placenta. Such rituals are becoming more common here; you can read a good overview by doula trainer Robin Elise Weiss at pregnancy.about.com/library/weekly/aa081302a.htm. If you want to see the placenta, ask. It's pretty amazing to see the only organ that the body produces and then discards.

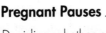

Pregnant Pauses

Deciding whether or not to circumcise your male newborn can be highly emotional, and influenced by faith, family tradition, or culture. Decide with your partner *before* the birth, and then don't let anyone shame you into believing you made a bad choice.

Apgar & Co.

Your child gets an Apgar test one minute after birth, and again five minutes after birth. This simple, effective diagnostic tool was invented in the early 1950s by anesthesiologist Virginia Apgar, M.D.

Dr. Apgar assigned each letter of her name to an important aspect of newborn health (she had a good knack for PR). On a scale of 0 (signs of trouble) to 2 (everything is rosy), a nurse or doctor will rate the following characteristics of your baby:

- **Appearance.** The color of the newborn's skin. Pink gets a 2 and blue a zero.
- **Pulse.** Baby gets a 2 for a pulse of more than 100 beats per minute.
- **Grimace.** The baby's reflexes are evaluated by his crying, response to stimulation, and irritability.
- **Activity.** Rating of how much the baby moves his arms and legs, an indication of muscle tone.
- **Respiration.** How regular is his breathing and does he cry without much effort.

Apgar is a time-saving, noninvasive tool for health-care pros to determine if the baby is getting enough oxygen or is under other undue stress.

A Change in Plans

Childbirth doesn't always go smoothly or according to expectations. Millions of factors must line up just right over the many months of pregnancy and there are some things that simply cannot be controlled or accounted for.

Fortunately, we live in a time and culture with frequent and incredible advances in obstetrics and neonatology for when childbirth doesn't follow nature's preferred pattern of labor and delivery.

Cesarean Sections

A cesarean section is surgery. The doctor opens up the mother's abdomen, then cuts into the uterus and lifts the baby out. As surgeries go, it's a fairly straightforward affair. After all, the surgeon knows just what he or she will find in there!

In the past, all cesarean sections were performed with the mother under general anesthesia and with dad out of the room. General anesthesia is still very common, but a woman can often have a spinal block instead, so she is awake when the baby is born.

It usually takes longer for a woman to recover from a cesarean than from vaginal childbirth. Her incision has to heal, and she'll face weeks of restrictions on lifting—which means you'll need to carry that load.

It is also common now for the expectant father to be in the operating room for a cesarean birth, so he can provide support and see and hold the newborn.

If you get good, consistent prenatal care, your OB/GYN will discern whether your partner is at risk for having trouble delivering vaginally. He or she may recommend a scheduled cesarean in order to head off danger to Mom and child.

A cesarean may also come into play if the fetus is in some sort of distress, and the mother hasn't reached full term or is not yet in active labor. It's not uncommon for premature babies to be delivered by cesarean.

If a woman's labor is stuck in stage one for many hours, and the OB/GYN is concerned about her health and/or the baby's, he or she may opt for an emergency cesarean. The surgery is also indicted when the baby is in a dangerous position inside the uterus, such as feet first.

No one likes to go the cesarean route, but it may be the only way to the ultimate goal.

Cesarean procedure has improved over the years, which is good news for you and your partner. Most of the time, the incision is so low on the abdomen that no scar will show when she is clothed (even in a bikini). The incisions are smaller, too, and done in a way that increases the odds that she can deliver vaginally next time she's pregnant—probably the most important improvement. Still, many doctors won't go that route, and if your partner has had two C-sections, she'll need one for any future birth.

Dad's Cesarean Role

A cesarean section, especially an emergency one, is scary for the expectant father (and mother). You know this isn't the way it's supposed to go, and realize that your partner and/or baby are in some degree of trouble. Plus, you know that major surgery is a risk in and of itself.

However, the vast majority of cesarean sections are successful and, by the standards of surgery, uneventful.

The professionals around you have done this many times before. Ask questions, but keep your eye on the goal, which is doing what's necessary in time.

Some hospitals won't let a father into the surgery at all. Others require you to take a cesarean preparation class, which you obviously can't do on the day of the surgery. So be sure to discuss the cesarean scenario with your OB/GYN and hospital ahead of time. If they aren't willing to let you into a cesarean, find another birthing team.

Crib Notes

Armin Brott, author of *The Expectant Father* (Abbeville Press, 2002), wisely warns that you "Never, never, never suggest to your pregnant partner that she consider a C-section—let your doctor make the first move." You may have the best intentions of sparing her hours of painful labor, but hold your tongue. Your partner is likely to think your suggestion completely undermines her cherished ideal of giving birth the "regular way."

Here's what to expect during a cesarean:

- You probably won't see your partner prepped for surgery.
- You will probably get much less attention from the professionals than during a vaginal

delivery. Don't get in the way, but make your presence known. Ask questions, politely and judiciously.

- You will probably be placed next to your partner's head, especially if she's awake for the surgery. Your job is to be the same supportive, encouraging, can't-wait-to-see-our baby guy you planned to be in the delivery room.

- If the baby doesn't have pressing medical needs, insist that you hold him and, if possible, give him to your partner for nursing.

- Cut the cord. You should discuss this with the OB/GYN beforehand, but there's no reason you can't cut the umbilical cord after a successful cesarean.

Breech Birth

Breech birth describes a baby who is not in position to exit head first from the uterus (there are several varieties of breech positions). Head first is the least problematic path, since that's what all the physiology is set up to handle. But life, and childbirth, doesn't always work that way.

An OB/GYN can try to manipulate the baby into a better position by reaching up the birth canal and/ or by maneuvering the mother's body. If that doesn't work, you can be pretty sure you're headed to the operating room for a cesarean.

The Least You Need to Know

- Dad is the primary advocate, coach, and comforter all the way through delivery.

- Participate as fully as you can in the birth by delivering the baby and cutting the cord, if possible.

- You should be a part of a cesarean birth.

- Prepare for what you want during delivery, and prepare to adapt to circumstances that arise.

Chapter **10**

Expecting the Unexpected

In This Chapter

- When things go wrong
- Dealing with miscarriage or infant death
- Twinning ways

Before I had children, I chuckled when people said: "You'll never know what it's like to have a kid until you have a kid." I felt sure they were exaggerating—until I had kids.

No one is ever completely prepared to raise this one individual child who emerges from the womb. I had identical twins, and there were still many days (including today) when it took two entirely different sets of fathering skills to relate successfully with each of them.

There are any number of traits and issues that you simply cannot anticipate ahead of time. That's a little nerve-wracking when you dwell on it, but it's also what makes fathering a thrilling, evolving adventure. (My kids are adults, and I'm still learning how to be their dad.)

While you know intellectually that you don't know who your baby will be, it's a rare expectant dad who doesn't fantasize about playing catch with his son or canoeing with his daughter. As it turns out, some of us end our delivery day with both a daughter and a son—and perhaps even another child or two.

And some of us have children who can't paddle or play catch, as much as they and we wish that they could.

Some of our kids are born with genetic abnormalities, diseases, or other problems. Some of our kids die in infancy or never survive in the womb. These are hard realities to acknowledge, and hard realities to live through as a dad.

Crib Notes

Remember this: Nearly all men who live through the most trying fathering challenges will tell you that their lives, and the lives of those around them, are richer and more interesting than they ever were before. Why? Because it's a wondrous, life-altering experience when a man has a child, no matter who that child turns out to be.

This chapter tells you briefly about some of these challenges (some happy and some not), as well as where to go for more information.

Miscarriage and Infant Death

Miscarriage means that the embryo or fetus does not survive until birth. Most miscarriages happen early in pregnancy; the chance of miscarriage decreases as the pregnancy progresses. Infant death is the death of a child during the first few hours, days, or months after birth.

For nearly all women who miscarry or give birth to a sick child, it happens just by chance. Nothing the parents did or didn't do during pregnancy caused it and it's not their fault. Literally millions of chemical and biological sequences must happen in the right order for an embryo or fetus to survive pregnancy and an infant to survive the early days of life. It's remarkable that these tragedies don't happen more often. Plus, improvements in health care and standard of living have reduced the number of miscarriages and infant deaths in many countries.

Miscarriages are caused by genetics, hormones, serious infections, anatomic abnormalities, and other, rarer issues. In nearly every case, these are things that you and your partner cannot control. You can read more about the types of miscarriage and their causes in many of the comprehensive pregnancy books available.

However, when it comes to expectant fathers, the biggest problem in miscarriage and infant death is grief. Both are deeply sad experiences. Unfortunately, many people minimize your loss because *they* never saw the baby; she was not "real" to them. But the baby was real to you, whether or not she was born, and this may complicate your own sense of grief.

Pregnant Pauses

The hundreds of books about pregnancy and childbirth can provide you with great detail about every conceivable (no pun intended) problem and abnormality that could arise. My friend William says, "My wife got so freaked out by one of those books that she threw it against the wall and screamed in frustration." Reading about all the problematic possibilities may trigger fear and anxiety, so keep your perspective and use those resources judiciously.

Your Loss Is Real

There should be no shame attached to infant death or miscarriage, because you did nothing wrong. For example, despite what you hear, expectant parents can't cause a miscarriage or birth defect by having sex, getting exercise, sleeping in a certain position, or eating spicy food.

You have every right to grieve, as does your partner and the rest of the family. However, you must realize that you and your partner may grieve this loss (or any loss) in different ways. Some say that the mother grieves more because she carried and felt the baby inside her. But advances in technology now allow an expectant dad to see, hear, and sense the baby before birth, too.

However, surviving a miscarriage or child's death is not a matter of "keeping score" about who grieves "more" than whom. There is no way to compare, even if comparing was the point (which it isn't). It *is* a matter of understanding how you are expressing your grief, and understanding that your partner will probably express hers differently.

Can Dad Be Sad?

Women often complain that men are socialized to "hide" their inner feelings. I don't buy that description. I think we men always reveal our feelings, but are socialized not to do it directly. The result? We have trouble expressing our feelings in a way that helps us or our loved ones understand those feelings (and us).

You may express your grief by burying yourself in your job, house projects, drinking, marathon TV watching, or other behaviors that keep you in isolation. You may rebel at the thought of joining (or attending even one meeting of) a support group for parents who lost a child. You may grow weary of your partner's tears and other expressions of sadness, and be impatient to "move on."

Silent isolation and impatience do three things:

- Keep you from processing your own feelings and thoughts.
- Keep you from moving healthily forward in life.
- Send your partner (and others) a signal that you didn't care as much about the baby as she did.

The Marriage After

Both the death of a child after birth and miscarriage put serious strain on a marriage or marriagelike relationship. It's easy to see why; you are each under strain, and you may have trouble understanding each other's response to the trauma.

One father who belongs to a support group for parents of miscarriage put it like this: "Life after a miscarriage will ultimately draw you closer together, or drive you further apart."

Drawing on suggestions from The March of Dimes and the British Website Women's Health Information, here are some steps to help you grieve and to help your relationship stay strong:

- Be caring about each other, your feelings, and your needs.
- Keep an open line of communication and share your thoughts and emotions.
- Accept your differences and acknowledge each other's pain.
- Assure one another of your commitment to your relationship.
- Talk about your baby and find ways to remember him or her.

Death and loss are difficult things to talk about. Most people are afraid of death and try to deny it. Therefore, they sometimes say or do stupid or insensitive things to a grieving parent, even if their intentions are good.

Pregnant Pauses

It's hard to get "too much" help and support after a miscarriage or infant death. There's great online advice from the March of Dimes (www.marchofdimes. com), The Arc (www.thearc.org), National Institutes of Health (www.nih.gov), and the UK's Women's Health Information (www. womens-health.co.uk/miscarr.htm). You can also find more information on birth defects on these sites.

In your desire to comfort yourself, your partner, or your family, you may fall into the same trap. Here are some important things *not* to do or say to your partner—or yourself:

- Let your anger or sadness stop you from getting support and love.

- "We can always have another child to replace this one." You may have more children, but there is no "replacement" for this particular child you created together.

- Be afraid to talk openly with family and friends about your loss.

- "You/I/we shouldn't feel sad anymore." If you are open about your grief and get support, you will move on. But this loss will always be sad.

- Blame the miscarriage or infant death on yourself or your partner. It wasn't your fault, and there's already enough guilt after such a loss.

- Pretend this didn't happen to you, or that it's no big deal. Don't let your family and friends pretend this either.

Think of it this way: If your father died this Friday, no one (including you) would expect you back at work on Monday morning with all your feelings swept away, and arrangements tidied up as if nothing had happened. So don't expect something different when you've just lost a child, even if it's one you never saw or held.

Miscarriage and infant death are real losses that bring real grief, anger, frustration, and feelings of helplessness. Some parents describe it as losing the potential within a life they hoped to share with their child. This real loss has real feelings *for the father and mother both*. Respect the loss and honor your baby by taking your grief seriously.

Twins, Triplets, and More

In the United States, about 1 in every 34 pregnancies produces twins. Fraternal twins are siblings no different than kids born years apart; each child has a unique genetic makeup. That's because they come from two different fertilized eggs inside Mom. Despite the male adjective, fraternal twins can be two girls, two boys, or one of each.

Identical twins come from a single fertilized egg that splits early in pregnancy, for reasons scientists have yet to nail down. That means identical twins have the same genetic code (thus, you get only one gender: two boys or two girls). As the father of twins, rest assured that the science of twins pales alongside the chaos of trying to manage more than one infant at a time.

Triplets, quadruplets, and other so-called "higher order multiple births" are most common among older women and women who take fertility drugs. As you might imagine, multiple fetuses take up a lot of room in a uterus, giving them extra incentive to get the heck out of there. That's why many multiples are born prematurely and are more likely to be born by cesarean. However, due to medical advances, far more "multiples" survive childbirth and infancy than ever before.

Crib Notes

According to the National Center for Health Statistics, during 1999, about 1 in every 34 U.S. pregnancies produces twins. About 1 in every 540 U.S. pregnancies resulted in 3 or more babies, or what statisticians call "higher order multiples." Whoever decided to put "higher order" and triplets in the same sentence obviously never had a set—"higher chaos," maybe.

Twins and other "multiples" tend to be physically smaller than other children (known as "singletons" in twin world slang). Many remain smaller all their lives, and sometimes one twin is smaller than the

other. It's not uncommon for a multiple to fall behind singletons in development of language skills,
although that usually doesn't reflect on their intelligence.

Crib Notes

If you have multiples, the place to go
for tips and support is the National Organization of Mothers of Twins Clubs: www.
nomotc.org, PO Box 438, Thompsons
Station, TN 37179-0438, 877-540-
2200. Yes, the "Mothers" part drives me
batty, too. But they have good information,
and include local chapters called, more
appropriately, "Parents of Multiples Clubs."

Our daughters are identical twins, but we didn't
know there were two until a few hours before they
were born. Sonograms weren't so common then,
but Nancy's water broke three weeks early, and the
doctor was trying to figure out why. In came a crusty,
veteran OB nurse (she also happened to be a nun)
who took one look at Nancy's belly and said, "If that's
one baby, it's a mighty big one." Sister went out in
the hall and told the doctor, "She's having twins."

The doctor took a quick x-ray, and we were informed,
to quote exactly, "Honey, it's two!" In shock, Nancy
argued with the doctor, who responded, "There's
nothing we can do about it now." A logical answer,
but not very comforting to first-time parents with
only one car seat!

Fortunately, the birth went smoothly, and we soon found that people reached out to us with offers of help. Friends and family sent hand-me-down clothes, strollers, money for a second car seat, and (best of all) my sister and brother-in-law gave us two free months of diaper service.

If you have multiples, you need to ask for and accept the help and kindness of friends and family. It also means a radical adjustment in your schedule, because no parent can manage more than one infant alone; not for more than a few hours, anyway. My wife and I both went to work part time, on "opposite" schedules, so that one of us was with the kids. It was chaotic at times, but well worth it.

The Least You Need to Know

- Miscarriages and infant deaths are not your fault.
- You can feel sad and angry about a problem, and still love your child.
- Start early to provide for children if you're gone.
- If you have multiples, be prepared for a lot of work and support.

11

Be Your Own Kind of Dad

In This Chapter

- Tuning your baby antenna
- A few words for Mom
- Gatekeeping and you
- Provider predicaments
- Free to father

Sooner or later, you'll bring your newborn back home with you. That's an exciting and scary day. There's no going back now; despite what your Great Uncle Harry used to threaten, you can't return a kid to the hospital for a refund.

The birth of your baby is burned into your memory forever. Now, dozens of memories will be created every day, as you participate in the miracle of your child's growth and development. It's unlikely you've ever had someone be so completely dependent on you before, and it's quite wonderful to feel so needed—and to provide so much to her.

Of course, with each day, your baby inches toward her adulthood when she can have babies of her own, if she wants. That's the ultimate paradox of fathering: You provide and nurture your baby (and the deep bond you're establishing with her), at the same time that you prepare her to eventually leave you.

I was sad the day we dropped our last daughter off to start college. Longing to hang on just a little bit longer, I gave her numerous hugs as she raced through orientation and set up her dorm room. Finally, she shooed us to the front door, where I reached out for one more hug. She held up her hand, pointed to the door and said, "Yes, Dad, I love you. Now go away."

 Crib Notes

> Wait until there's an infant in your house. The first six months, I was ready to go to bed at 8—and a surprising number of nights, that really was bedtime. Basically, everything is going to change, even during the pregnancy, and there's a huge range of things that fit in the "normal" category. Be reassured that most things are temporary. Take each day as it comes.
>
> —Chris

That may be the best compliment I ever got on my fathering. By the time she'd finished her childhood, my child was sure that she loved me, and that I mattered to her. She was also sure that she had what it takes to live her life independently of me. As my wife and I drove home, I realized: "That's been my goal from the day we brought our babies home."

It's a good goal to aim for. This chapter will give you some hints on how to think about your fathering style, so you can get from day one to the day of farewell.

Tuning In the Infant Channel

Guess what? Your life will never be the same again, even if you already have kids. Now that this individual child has entered your life, the two of you will reveal miraculous new things about yourselves to each other on a regular basis.

The first amazing thing you'll learn is how instinctively you can communicate with each other, even though it'll be a year or more before he'll have many words to use. The late pediatric psychologist Lee Salk (brother of Jonas, creator of the polio vaccine) urged parents to trust this kind of natural connection.

Salk's *What Every Child Would Like His Parents to Know* (Warner, 1973, now out of print), comforted me as a new dad worried about whether I was up for the job. Ironically for a parenting author, Salk said not to put too much stock in the latest parenting book. He wisely encouraged me to trust my heart and my baby's sounds and body. If I tuned in to the channel my infant was "broadcasting" on, I'd have much of the information I'd need to be a good father.

Of course, it would be foolish to rely on instinct alone when there are fabulous resources available for "beginner" fathers, like *The New Father: A Dad's Guide to the First Year* by Armin A. Brott (Abbeville Press, 1997) and *What to Expect the First Year* by Arlene Eisenberg, et. al. (Workman, 2003).

We don't have space here to give great detail about early childhood development, but then a 26-volume encyclopedia on the subject would just scratch the surface! Good books and websites give you general guidelines on what to expect developmentally, and share the insights of experts—the everyday parents who have been there before you.

The two best things a "new parent" resource can do is to:

- Give you some bricks for your fathering foundation, and a few panes of glass for the walls.

- Encourage you to build your own unique greenhouse in which to raise a vibrant, lush, and well-rooted child.

Crib Notes

There's no harm in a child crying: the harm is done only if his cries aren't answered. If you ignore a baby's signal for help, you don't teach him independence. What you teach him is that no other human being will take care of his needs.

—Dr. Lee Salk

The Only Part of This Book That Mom *Has* to Read

Put the book down for a minute, and go get your partner for a brief lesson on culture, gender, and parenting. No, really, go get her now. I'll wait.

Are you both back now? Okay, here's what you need to know:

Our culture effectively (through both subtle and blatant practices) places the domain of child-rearing almost exclusively in the hands of the mother. Even in families fully committed to shared parenting, the mother often becomes the gatekeeper of child-rearing.

She usually does the feeding, schedules the sitter, instructs Dad and babysitter on the proper way to change diapers, and is the redoubt of last resort when the baby won't stop crying. Dad defers because that's what he's supposed to do; he's no expert—and who isn't tempted to bypass a dirty diaper?

The Invisible Gatekeeper

Let me be absolutely clear: Mothers and fathers do *not* fall into these gatekeeping patterns in order to get back at each other, win a power struggle, or because one loves the children more than the other. Not at all. It happens because we grew up in a world that taught us to divvy up parenting responsibilities by gender.

Most of the time, moms take on the gatekeeper role (and fathers forfeit it) unconsciously and with the best intentions. The arrangement may seem logical. Go back to your respective teenage baby-sitting resumes, and you'll probably find that Dad has much less experience than Mom with feeding, burping, and rocking a baby to sleep. But a Mother-knows-best model only looks "logical" if you accept some pretty screwy cultural notions about gender roles in society.

Screwy notion number one is that child-rearing is women's work. Close behind is screwy notion number two to suggest that men don't "do" child-rearing; they're supposed to bread-win and look proudly upon their kiddies from afar.

Don't get me wrong; child-rearing *is* women's work. But it's also *men's* work. The default cultural standards leave Dad out, which makes more work for Mom, and leaves everyone in the family father hungry—and that's what's screwy. (Don't go away, Mom, there are a few more paragraphs for you to read.)

Daddy Can't Breast-Feed

Daddy can't breast-feed? Duh. Fathers have never breast-fed their children, and probably never will (if nature has her way). Breast-feeding is a miraculous natural feat that brings concrete benefits to Mother and child spiritually, emotionally, and physically. It brings some vicarious benefits to Dad, too.

But breast-feeding can be the first place where parents fall into the powerful, seductive (and often invisible) pattern of Mom as gatekeeper and Dad as ancillary.

An eager new father seldom feels more like he's on the outside looking in than when his partner is breast-feeding their child. That's one responsibility and opportunity that Dad simply cannot accomplish. It's also a situation that often seems taboo to discuss. After all, who wants to be against breast-feeding and motherhood?

Pregnant Pauses

Here's a father's reflection from Le Leche League International's magazine New Beginnings (www.lalecheleague.org/NB/NBfathers.html):

> Everything we learned about breast-feeding was tremendously helpful during those first few intense weeks. I'm sure there is a primal urge that drives a parent to want their child to eat. I remember watching Ileana trying to get Alex to latch on the very first day. When he did it, a tremendous sense of relief came over me that suddenly turned to panic when he broke off and had to start over. Thankfully, Alex and Ileana figured things out quickly.
>
> —Jim

Don't worry, a father who looks longingly on while his partner nourishes their infant is not against breast-feeding or motherhood. When my wife

Nancy breast-fed our daughters, I felt proud and amazed. But I simultaneously felt left out and fervently wished that there was something more I could do in the crucial, recurring responsibility of feeding the babies.

Open the Gates and Feed

During the first six weeks of being parents, Nancy struggled through a grueling schedule of trying to get two weak-sucking preemies to eat enough to be strong enough to suck enough to eat enough to be strong enough … a vicious cycle. I got up in the night to bring her the babies, waited on her while she fed, and cheered from the sidelines. But none of it felt adequate.

Finally, Nancy felt too exhausted to keep going. With the doctor's approval, we switched to bottles. I was sad that she wouldn't get to fully enjoy breast-feeding, but also thrilled that I could now feed the girls (and that Nancy wouldn't be so worn out anymore).

From then on, each of us got to hold a daughter close to our chest, snuggling, kissing, and cooing while we fed. I felt my connection with my daughters deepen immediately. It still wasn't easy for either of us to coax them into eating enough to be strong enough to eat enough on their own—but at least I could take on half of the battle.

You don't have to do it they way we did. In fact, if breast-feeding is working well, you shouldn't interrupt it. But the two of you also have to find creative ways to include Dad in the feeding process—and other current and future routine infant care duties.

Here are some ideas for *both* of you:

- Mom breast-feeds, and Dad burps the baby.
- Once the baby can handle it without disrupting breast-feeding, pump Mom's milk for a bottle, so that dad can feed, too. This builds dad-baby intimacy, and gives mom a break.
- When baby is not eating, Dad holds him, plays with him, and puts him to sleep just as often as Mom does (or even a little bit more).
- If Dad is holding a baby who won't stop crying, dad gets (and takes) the time and space to figure out his solution.
- Advise and encourage; don't hover.
- Think before you "rescue." You both have plenty to learn about this child. Your children teach you every day that many important lessons come from mistakes. Don't keep each other from your mistakes. (A good attitude to have with your kids, too, when they're older.)

Remember that the two of you may have different ways of feeding, burping, and changing your baby. You may have different ways of playing with him or getting him to drop off to sleep.

This is a *good* thing!

For example, some research indicates that a father is more likely to carry an infant so that she is facing away from him, while a mother is more likely to carry the baby facing toward her. Your baby needs both perspectives. It's good for her to explore the

world and it's good for her to know her family intimately. It doesn't matter which parent provides
which—and it's probably best if both parents provide both.

The key is to remember that an infant has more
than one parent for very good reasons. Don't let
either parent be locked out, because that's not
good for the child.

Dads and moms, look out for gatekeeping. Talk
openly when either of you think it's happening.
And don't fall into blaming; gatekeeping doesn't
happen unless you both let it happen. By the same
token, both parents are responsible for sharing the
obligations, opportunities, and joys of raising their
children.

Okay, Mom, you can go back to what you were
doing before. Unless you're so captivated by the
author's amazing writing that you simply must go
back to page one and read everything. (No? It's
okay; I won't take it personally.)

Diapering Your Way to Daddydom

In movies and sitcoms, you'll often see a father run
screaming from the room is there's a diaper to be
changed or spit-up to be cleaned up. It's a quick,
cheap laugh, but it belittles fathers—and the most
surefire way to build a strong relationship with
your child.

Do the dirty work. Change the diapers, give the
baths, wipe up the puke. These are the jobs we do
in the workshop of fathering.

Here is how we build our relationship with our children: by babbling, tickling, making eye contact, singing, making faces, wiping butts, snuggling, kissing, comforting, and falling asleep together in the rocking chair. Your baby doesn't do these things on a predictable schedule, so neither can you. You have to be there when it happens. Of course, that means doing the work-family balancing act. The U.S. Family and Medical Leave Act provides marginal help, requiring up to 12 weeks unpaid leave for the birth of a child—but only if you've worked more than a year for a company with more than 50 employees. A few companies and state governments offer better family leave, but most employees who use it are women. Men still believe (often with good reason) that their career and/or job reputation will suffer if they take leave. Instead, they cobble together sick days and vacation to attend special family events. It really is sick that managers and peers still think a man is somehow "weak" or lacks "loyalty" by showing commitment to his family.

Bosses who get their heads out of their Neanderthal prejudices can see how support for father involvement actually *improves* worker productivity and the bottom line. When an employer helps a man be present in his family, that man is less likely to get sick and is more likely to stay with his job. Cutting down on sick days and employee turnover is money in the bank to any employer.

Since we and our fellow males still hold the vast majority of leadership and policy-making positions in the workplace, there's a lot we can do to promote work-family balance. If you are a manager, start lobbying for policies to help fathers (and mothers) be deeply involved in their children's lives. If the higher-ups are fathers themselves, lobby them to recognize the benefits of work-family balance for all parties.

Dads and Dollars

Broaden your definition of "provider." A father often thinks that he must provide for his child primarily by delivering a paycheck, even if that means working so long and hard that he seldom sees his child. Good fathering *does* require providing money, but just as important, it requires providing ourselves: our time, experience, masculinity, affection, and more.

In my book *Dads and Daughters: How to Inspire, Support and Understand Your Daughter* (Broadway, 2003), I wrote that one of the biggest hurdles facing fathers is "the provider predicament." It's a feeling that we must bring home as much bacon as possible, even if it means we and our kids don't know each other very well.

This way of thinking requires a significant trade-off that we seldom address squarely. To meet that relentless economic provider expectation, we usually spend more time, energy and attention away from home (and our kids) than their mothers do.

Our fatherly impact is in the details of life. Think of all the looks exchanged and words we speak every time we change a diaper; the affection we show when we walk the midnight floor calming a colicky baby; or the pride we convey by listening to our daughter read her first books. Our greatest opportunity to deepen and strengthen our relationships with our children lies in the never-ending, mundane (often boring and monotonous) daily caring for those children.

Not too many of us have fathers who took on a big share of diaperlike duties. Most of our parents were waylaid by that screwy "this is women's work" mindset. But fathering today is different. There is great and growing support for greater father involvement.

That means we can (and should) create new ways of fathering. We can brainstorm with other fathers (and mothers), learn from their experiences, and lend them a hand. (Of course, that means we have to talk to each other …)

Here are just a handful of ways fathers are redefining the best job a man ever had:

- Being a stay-at-home dad, being the primary parent.
- Volunteering for Head Start programs, Brownie troops, Cub Scout packs, PTAs, etc.
- Letting each child pick a day (it could even be a school day) to go somewhere of her choosing to spend the day with Dad.

- Making career decisions based on how much support the job gives fathers for spending time with their families.

- Making career decisions based on how close the workplace is to where one's children live (something *many* divorced pro athletes do nowadays).

- Making household chores (cooking, laundry, dusting, etc.) part of Dad's daily routine.

Dads and Dollars

My dad participated in the Saturday chore day, so I never viewed my mom as the "homemaker" and Dad as *just* the bread winner. I also remember that my dad loved to bake us cookies once or twice a month, and he'd have all four kids help him. He's famous for his cookies where he works, and it makes me feel good to know that his students get his cookies now that us kids are grown. I have fond memories of my dad and mom for the people they were and the little details of my upbringing. I have no idea how much money either of them made during my childhood. I just know they were at my T-ball games, they took us fishing, and they didn't parent by the gender roles that were "expected" of them.

—Ginny

You read this book because you want to be have a central role in the pregnancy you and your partner are sharing, and you want to be a key player on the first day of your child's life. That involved approach lays the groundwork for being a wonderful dad.

I call it having "Lamaze intensity" about pregnancy and childbirth. You're willing to go to classes, protect and nurture your partner, make sacrifices, and go joyously thorough the chaotic miracle of labor and delivery.

Your next challenge is to take your Lamaze intensity into every day of your new baby's childhood. Your child needs you that involved. He needs *you* to show him how to hug, bake cookies, snowshoe, and be a man. She needs *you* to show her how to drive a nail, jump off the high dive, tie a lure, and how a good man loves a woman.

Fathering is too good an experience for you or your child to miss. So please, show up for it every day. You'll be amazed before you're halfway through.

Pregnant Pauses

I look at my children now and notice their eyes and expressions. It brings me back to when I first held each of them. I loved to see them peeking up at me from the cuddly blanket. They were/are so beautiful. You'll see!!!

—Tom

Those of us who already have children welcome you into the fraternity of fathers. We are honored to have you in our fellowship. May you cherish your membership every day.

The Least You Need to Know

- Fathers have child-rearing instincts they can trust.
- Raising kids is fathers' work.
- Learn how to recognize and defuse "gate-keeping."
- Act like you're more than a paycheck, because you are.
- Be an involved, committed father; bring "Lamaze intensity" to every fathering day.

Appendix

Glossary

active labor   The period of regular contractions that leads up to delivery.

advocate   Central role for expectant fathers; standing up for your partner and you.

alcohol   Responsible for more addiction than all other drugs combined. Pregnant women should avoid it and Dad's shared abstinence makes this much easier.

anxiety   Normal feeling for expectant fathers, who worry whether they'll do the job well enough.

Apgar   Simple test done immediately after birth to determine the baby's health. Apgar is the acronym for the things the test measures: appearance, pulse, grimace (reflexes), activity, and respiration.

attunement   Using awareness, listening, and instinct to tune in to your child's feelings, thoughts, and needs.

birth center   Nonhospital setting for birth, often staffed by midwives.

birth plans   Written list of your wishes for the labor, childbirth, and post-delivery experience. All your care providers should have a copy, and you should be prepared to alter the plan if needed for safety of your partner or baby.

Bradley Method Childbirth method that relies on breathing, internal focus, and central involvement of the birth coach (you!).

Braxton Hicks contractions "False" contractions that prepare the uterus in the days/weeks before active labor.

breast pump Device that pumps breast milk for use in bottle feeding.

breast-feeding Provides nutrition and immunity for a newborn. Preferred method of feeding, although bottle feeding can also produce healthy children.

breech birth When the baby's head is not "presenting" at the birth canal, thus requiring manipulation and/or surgery for a safe delivery.

cesarean section Surgery to remove the baby when vaginal birth is not possible or safe.

certified nurse midwife (CNM) Trained in pregnancy, labor, and delivery, CNMs usually offer more relaxed, attentive childbirth environments.

cervix Tissue that holds the bottom of the uterus closed, then thins and opens during labor.

child safety seat Required by state law, it protects children in vehicles.

childbirth education classes Essential in preparing for birth. Attend them!

chronic sorrow Normal sad response to miscarriage, infant death, or birth defects.

coach One who supports, guides, and advocates for a woman during pregnancy and childbirth.

commitment level   You prove your commitment and involvement level (to yourself, partner, and baby) by how much attention and time you dedicate.

communication   Listening, speaking, tuning in to your partner's needs. The single most essential tool in pregnancy and child rearing.

contractions   Tightening of muscles around the uterus that eventually help push the baby out at birth. You should track them and handle one at a time.

cooking, cleaning, laundering   You must learn them in order to be a truly involved father.

Couvade syndrome   Real physical and psychological symptoms expectant fathers have during pregnancy, such as food cravings and nausea.

crowning   The moment when the first part of the baby appears; much more time may pass before full delivery.

cutting the cord   An opportunity many fathers take to more fully participate in childbirth and to bond with their newborns.

diagnostic tests   Throughout pregnancy (especially early) tests of you and your partner can help detect potential problems.

diapering   Father's work. Mundane tasks, such as diapering, are when you build your relationship with your child.

diet/nutrition   The appropriate diet to keep your partner healthy during pregnancy. Help your partner eat well and follow doctor's orders by cooking and eating the same food she does and cheering her on.

dilation Thinning of the cervix, and widening of the cervical opening.

doula Experienced, trained advocate who helps Mom and Dad through labor and delivery.

dreaming It's common for expectant fathers to dream about their unborn children. Enjoy the dreams, but don't take them literally.

due dates An estimate of delivery day; don't put too much stock in these.

false contractions *See* Braxton-Hicks.

family and friends Learn from them, involve them, rely on them, but don't let them take over your central responsibility for your partner and child.

family history Illnesses and genetic traits that appear in your family or origin and/or ancestors. Share your family medical history with your OB/GYN, and learn lessons from its parenting history.

going to the hospital too soon Better too soon than too late; don't be embarrassed to go to or call the hospital when you feel it's time.

guardian Person legally named to raise a child if her parents die or are disabled.

gynecologist Physician specializing in health of the female reproductive system.

induction Use of synthetic hormones or other methods to trigger active labor and speed time of delivery.

infant death Death of a child in the days, weeks, or months following birth.

instinct   Nature's most effective tool for helping parents through pregnancy and beyond.

intimacy   The deep connection between people, especially parenting partners. Intimacy is verbal, emotional, physical, and spiritual.

Lamaze   Childbirth method that relies on breathing, external focus, and central involvement of the birth coach (you!).

Leboyer   Childbirth method that uses low lights, reduced noise, and/or water tub for delivery.

leucorrhea   Vaginal discharge during pregnancy; normal in moderation.

miscarriage   Pregnancy that ends before childbirth with the death of the fetus.

morning sickness   Nausea and related symptoms that can happen at any time of day; some women have it all through pregnancy, others seldom if at all.

natural childbirth   A term usually used to describe childbirth without pain medication. All childbirth than produces a living baby and mother is natural.

nature   Millennia worth of fatherly experience in having and raising children; trust it.

neonatology   The study and medical treatment of newborns.

nesting instinct   Normal instinct of expectant fathers and mothers to ready the home for the newborn.

new family class   Offered by hospitals and other agencies to learn tips about caring for an infant.

normal In pregnancy and child-rearing, there is no normal. Your experience will be similar to many others', but also unique to you.

nursery The space in your home where your newborn sleeps; make it safe for baby and convenient for you.

nurturing A key responsibility of fathers in their relationships with partners and children.

OB/GYN or obstetrician Physician specializing in pregnancy and childbirth.

ovary Female organ where eggs are stored and released monthly.

paternity establishment Done through legal documents at birth and/or genetic testing, establishing paternity is essential for maintaining a father's rights and responsibilities, especially outside of marriage.

patience Key trait for expectant fathers before and after birth; exercise it often.

physician Keep your personal physician part of the process, making sure you stay in optimal health.

placenta Miraculous organ that feeds the fetus in the womb, then is delivered from the uterus after the baby.

pregnancy Starts when the zygote attaches to the uterine wall and ends when the fetus is born.

pregnancy books Can be helpful, but their level of detail (especially about potential problems) can also create anxiety. Use them judiciously as guides.

preparing the home Wonderful way for you to share the pregnancy excitement with your partner.

provider   A father's role includes providing more than money. You must also provide your time, experience, affection, masculinity, chores, enthusiasm, etc.

sharing the news   Tell people about your pregnancy when you want to, but be sure you're on the same page as your partner.

smoking   If you have or are having children, don't smoke.

sonogram   *See* ultrasound.

sperm   Male reproductive cells that must enter a female egg for pregnancy to begin.

strong and silent   Not a good mode for fathers. Speak up, listen, share—this is what facilitates good fathering.

support/support groups   Ask for support from friends, family, your partner, and veteran dads. Parenting support groups offer a lot.

surrogate mothering   When a woman carries another couple's embryo in her womb and gives birth to the baby.

swelling   As pregnancy progresses, most women experience uncomfortable or painful swelling of feet, breasts, legs, etc.

testes   The male reproductive organ that produces sperm.

tough guise   The "tough" exterior that keeps many men from connecting fully with their partners and children.

transition from man to father What you experience while expecting; a good time to explore what kind of father you want to be.

transportation Establish primary and back-up plans for getting to the hospital at least two months before your due dates.

ultrasound Diagnostic tool using radio waves to determine growth and health of fetus.

umbilical cord Connects placenta to fetus, providing all nutrition.

unmarried fathers Usually don't have as many rights as married dads; make specific arrangements to address this.

uterus Female reproductive organ that holds the embryo and fetus.

vagina Expandable female organ that receives sperm, and later becomes the birth canal

veteran dads Fathers who already have children, they are great guides and supporters for you.

wills Adjust your will to reflect your new status as a father with children.

zygote The result of a fertilized egg, it attaches to the uterine wall to begin pregnancy.

Resources

Need some more help or need more information on a specific topic? The following resources will be of good help.

Pregnancy—General Information

- The Cleveland Clinic: Great, basic information and guidance:
  www.clevelandclinic.org/health/search/
  show-documents.
  asp?mediaID=5&topicId= 489&sortId=2

- Childbirth.org: Provides a lot of general information on child birth:
  www.Childbirth.org

- The Pregnancy Web Ring: a "ring" of many sites dedicated to pregnancy
  www.fensende.com/Users/swnymph/Ring.html

- American Pregnancy Association:
  1425 Greenway Drive, Suite 440
  Irving, TX 75038
  1-800-672-2296
  www.americanpregnancy.org

- Fetal development, illustrated in pictures: www.paternityangel.com/PicsAndPhotos/FoetalDevelop/DevInPics.htm

- Chart of pregnancy week by week: www.babycentre.co.uk/calendar/index?week=1

- Maternity Center Association: www.maternitywise.org

- National Institute on Alcohol Abuse and Alcoholism: www.niaaa.nih.gov/faq/faq.htm

- National Organization on Fetal Alcohol Syndrome: 1-800-66-NOFAS www.nofas.org

- National Clearinghouse for Alcohol and Drug Information: www.health.org

- "Nutrition During Pregnancy": To order this free pamphlet, send a self-addressed, stamped, business-size envelope to: American College of Obstetricians and Gynecologists Resource Center/APOOI 409 12th St. SW Washington, D.C. 20024-2188

- *All About Sex: A Family Resource on Sex and Sexuality:* Planned Parenthood (Three Rivers Press, 1997)

- *What to Expect When Your Expecting:* Heidi Murkoff, Arlene Eisenberg, and Sandee Hathaway (Workman, 2002)

Expectant Fathers

- *The Expectant Father: Facts, Tips, and Advice for Dads-to-Be:* Armin Brott (Abbeville Press, 2002)

- Brand New Dads: An online community, resource center, and search engine for new and expectant fathers: www.brandnewdad.com

- The Expectant Father: One man's experience and resources: www.cyberfiles.com/expectantfather/contents.html

- Paternity Angel: A guide for expectant and new fathers: www.paternityangel.com

Single Fathers

- *The Single Father: A Dad's Guide to Parenting Without a Partner:* Armin Brott (Abbeville, 1999): A special volume for divorced, widowed, and gay dads

- New York Online Access to Health: Good information for new single fathers: www.noah-health.org/english/pregnancy/single.html

- Responsible Single Fathers: Provides mentoring, support and referrals to dads so they can cope, parent, nurture, love, and emotionally and financially care for their children: www.singlefather.org/

Finding the Right OB/GYN

- Cleveland Clinic: "Choosing an Obstetric Health Care Provider": www.clevelandclinic.org/health/ health-info/docs/2700/2795.asp?index=9698
- The American College of Obstetricians and Gynecologists: www.acog.org
- The Society of Obstetricians and Gynaecologists of Canada: Information in English and French: www.sogc.org/SOGCnet/
- Royal College of Obstetricians and Gynaecologists: www.rcog.org.uk
- The American College of Osteopathic Obstetricians and Gynecologists: www.acoog.com
- Society for Maternal-Fetal Medicine: 409 12th Street, SW Washington, D.C. 20024 202-863-2476 www.smfm.org

Doula, Midwife, and Other Alternatives

- The American College of Nurse-Midwives: www.acnm.org 202-728-9860

- Doulas of North America:
  www.dona.org,
  1-888-788-3662

- National Association of Childbearing Centers:
  www.birthcenters.org,
  215-234-8068

Getting Your Home Ready

- Consumer Product Safety Commission:
  guide to infant safety:
  www.cpsc.gov/CPSCPUB/PUBS/5025.pdf
  1-800-638-2772

- The National Highway Traffic Safety
  Administration:
  www.nhtsa.dot.gov/people/injury/childps/
  1-800-424-9393 (NHTSA Auto Safety
  Hotline)

- Virtual Children's Hospital: comprehensive
  material on the need for car seats:
  www.vh.org/pediatric/patient/pediatrics/
  cqqa/carseats.html

- The Juvenile Products Manufacturers
  Association:
  www.jmpa.org

- Family Shopping Guide to Car Seats: To order
  this free publication, send a self-addressed,
  stamped, business-size envelope to:
  The American Academy of Pediatrics
  Dept. C, PO Box 927
  Elk Grove Village, IL 60009-0927

- Finding the Best Care for Your Infant: To order a single free copy of this pamphlet, send a self-addressed, stamped, business-size envelope to: National Association for the Education of Young Children, 1509 16th St. NW, Number 518, Washington, D.C. 20036

Childbirth Classes

- Lamaze International: www.lamzae.org, 1-800-368-4404

- The Bradley Method: The American Academy of Husband-Coached Childbirth: www.bradleybirth.com, 1-800-422-4784

- American Society for the Alexander Technique: www.alexandertech.com/misc/pregnant.html

- The Association of Labor Assistants and Childbirth Educators: www.alace.org, 617-441-2500

- Association of Christian Childbirth Professionals: www.christianbirth.org

- Childbirth and Postpartum Professional Association: www.childbirthprofessional.com: 1-888-MY-CAPPA

- International Childbirth Education
  Association:
  www.icea.org
  612-854-8660

- Birthing from Within:
  www.birthpower.com
  505-254-4884

- LaLeche League International: promoting
  breast-feeding through support and education:
  www.lalecheleague.org/NB/NBfathers.html

- LaLeche League Canada:
  www.lalecheleaguecanada.ca

Legal and Financial Issues

- Birthfathers' Legal Rights: listing of State
  laws relative to the rights of putative fathers:
  www.calib.com/naic/laws/putative.cfm

- Social Security number for baby: You'll need
  to list your child's Social Security number
  on your tax return when claiming a depend-
  ency exemption for the child for the first full
  tax year after birth: Internal Revenue Service:
  www.irs.gov
  1-800-829-1040

Financial and Insurance Issues

- Met Life resources on implications of life transitions:
  www.metlife.com/Applications/Corporate/W PS/CDA/PageGenerator/
  0,1674,P785,00.html

- Medicare and Medicaid related topics:
  www.medicare.gov
  1-800-772-1213
  (Social Security Administration)

Gay Fathers

- *The Single Father: A Dad's Guide to Parenting Without a Partner:* Armin Brott (Abbeville, 1999): A special volume for divorced, widowed, and gay dads

- Lesbian and Gay Parenting: A Fact Sheet:
  www.lambdalegal.org/cgi-bin/iowa/
  documents/record?record=31

- Lambda Legal Foundation:
  120 Wall Street, Suite 1500
  New York, NY 10005-3904
  212-809-8585
  www.lambdalegal.org

Adoption

- National Adoption Information Clearinghouse:
  naic.acf.hhs.gov

- Adoptive Fathers:
  adoption.about.com/cs/adads/
- Extensive list of adoption resources:
  adoptions.adoption.com/
- Legal Issues of Independent Adoption:
  naic.acf.hhs.gov/pubs/f_legal.cfm#top#top
- *Adoption Is a Family Affair! What Relatives and Friends Must Know:* Patricia Irwin Johnston (Perspectives Press, 2001)
- *Launching a Baby's Adoption: Practical Strategies for Parents and Professionals:* Patricia Irwin Johnston (Perspectives Press, 1998)
- *Twenty Things Adopted Kids Wish Their Adoptive Parents Knew:* Sherrie Eldridge (Dell, 1999)

The Birth Plan

- IParenting.com guide (including samples) for creating a birth plan: birthplan.com

Labor and Delivery

- The Cleveland Clinic: "What to Expect During Labor":
  www.clevelandclinic.org/health/health-info/docs/0800/0848.asp?index=5283

- International Cesarean Awareness Network, Inc.:
  1304 Kingsdale Avenue
  Redondo Beach, CA 90278
  1-800-686-ICAN
  www.ican-online.org

- The Cleveland Clinic: "What to Pack for the Hospital":
  www.clevelandclinic.org/health/health-info/docs/2800/2843.asp?index=9678

- Placenta rituals: overview by doula trainer Robin Elise Weiss:
  pregnancy.about.com/library/weekly/aa081302a.htm

Miscarriage and Infant Death

- SIDS (Sudden Infant Death Syndrome): "Back to Sleep" Campaign:
  www.nichd.nih.gov/sids/

- Miscarriage Association of the United Kingdom:
  www.miscarriageassociation.org.uk/main3.htm

- Women's Health Information:
  www.womens-health.co.uk/miscarr.htm

- Medline Plus: from the U.S. National Library of Medicine:
  www.nlm.nih.gov/medlineplus/pregnancyloss.html

- The March of Dimes:
  www.marchofdimes.com/pnhec/572_4057.asp

- The Compassionate Friends:
  PO Box 3696
  Oak Brook, IL 60522-3696
  1-877-969-0010
  www.compassionatefriends.org

Birth Defects

- Fathers' Network: A website for fathers
  raising children with special health care
  needs and developmental disabilities:
  www.fathersnetwork.org

- The March of Dimes: the country's leading
  advocate on birth defects:
  www.marchofdimes.com
  1275 Mamaroneck Avenue
  White Plains, NY 10605
  e-mail: askus@marchofdimes.com

- The Arc of the United States:
  www.thearc.org
  1010 Wayne Avenue, Suite 650
  Silver Spring, MD 20910
  301-565-3842

- National Institutes of Health:
  www.nih.gov

- Women's Health Information:
  www.womens-health.co.uk/miscarr.htm

- National Down Syndrome Society:
  www.ndss.org
  666 Broadway
  New York, NY 10012
  1-800-221-4602

- Spina Bifida Association of America:
  www.sbaa.org
  4590 MacArthur Boulevard NW, Suite 250
  Washington, D.C. 20007-4226
  1-800-621-3141

- American Cleft Palate Foundation:
  www.cleftline.org
  104 South Estes Drive, Suite 204
  Chapel Hill, NC 27514
  1-800-24-CLEFT

- American Sickle Cell Anemia Association:
  www.ascaa.org
  10300 Carnegie Avenue
  Cleveland, OH 44106
  216-229-8600

- United Cerebral Palsy:
  www.ucp.org
  1660 L Street NW, Suite 700
  Washington, D.C. 20036
  1-800-872-5827

- *Playing the Hand That's Dealt to You:* Janel
  Morel (Canmore Press, 2000)

Twins, Triplets, and More

- National Organization of Mothers of Twins
  Clubs:
  www.nomotc.org
  PO Box 438
  Thompsons Station, TN 37179-0438
  1-877-540-2200

Parenting

- *The Courage to Raise Good Men: You Don't Have to Sever the Bond with Your Son to Help Him Become a Man:* Olga Silverstein (Penguin, 1995)

- *Reviving Ophelia: Saving the Selves of Adolescent Girls:* Mary Pipher (Ballentine, 1995)

- *Reviviendo a Ophelia (Reviving Ophelia en Espanol):* Mary Pipher (Downtown Book Center, Inc., 1997)

- Parent Soup: A wide assortment of parenting resources, free newsletter, etc.: www.parentsoup.com

- *Daughters: For Parents of Girls:* Bimonthly newsletter: www.daughters.com

- The National Black Child Development Institute: 1101 15th St NW, Suite 900 Washington, D.C. 20005 1-800-556-2234 www.nbcdi.org

- Parents' Place (including good sections on single parenting): www.parentsplace.com

- National Center for Early Development and Learning: www.fpg.unc.edu/~ncedl

- Family Education Network: fen.com/

- The Annie E. Casey Foundation: Building better futures for disadvantaged children and their families in the United States: www.aecf.org

New Fathers

- *The New Father: A Dad's Guide to the First Year*: Armin A. Brott (Abbeville Press, 1997)
- *What to Expect the First Year*: Arlene Eisenberg, et. al. (Workman, 2003)
- Baby development chart: www.babycentre.co.uk/general/6476.html
- The American Academy of Pediatrics: 141 Northwest Point Boulevard Elk Grove Village, IL 60007-1098 847-434-4000 www.aap.org
- "Understanding Fathering: The Early Head Start Study of Fathers of Newborns": Cheri A. Vogel, Kimberly Boller, Jennifer Faerber, Jacqueline D. Shannon, and Catherine S. Tamis-LeMonda: www.mathematica-mpr.com/PDFs/ redirect.asp?strSite=ehsnewborns.pdf
- Keep Kids Healthy: Dr. Vincent Iannelli's free pediatric parenting advice: www.keepkidshealthy.com

Fathering–General

- *Collected Wisdom of Fathers, The* : Will Glennon (Conari Press, 2002)

- *Father for Life: A Journey of Joy, Challenge, and Change:* Armin A. Brott (Abbeville Press, 2003)

- *Live-Away Dads: Staying a Part of Your Children's Lives When They Aren't a Part of Your Home:* William C. Klatte (Penguin, 1999)

- *Dads and Daughters: How to Inspire, Support and Understand Your Daughter:* Joe Kelly (Broadway Books, 2003)

- *Becoming Dad: Black Men and the Journey to Fatherhood:* Leonard Pitts (Longstreet Press, 1999)

- *Real Boys: Rescuing Our Sons from the Myths of Boyhood*: William S. Pollack (Owl Books, 1999)

- *200 Ways to Raise a Boy's Emotional Intelligence:* Will Glennon (Conari Press, 2000)

- *200 Ways to Raise a Girl's Self-Esteem:* Will Glennon (Conari Press, 1999)

- *Whatever Happened to Daddy's Little Girl?: The Impact of Fatherlessness on Black Women:* Jonetta Rose Barras (Random House, 2002)

- *The Single Father: A Dad's Guide to Parenting Without a Partner:* Armin A. Brott (Abbeville, 1999)

- *Faith of Our Fathers: African-American Men Reflect on Fatherhood:* Andre C. Willis (Editor), (Plume, 1997)

- *Throwaway Dads: The Myths and Barriers That Keep Men from Being the Fathers They Want to Be:* Armin Brott and Ross Parke (Houghton Mifflin, 1999)

- *Covering Home: Lessons on the Art of Fathering from the Game of Baseball:* Jack Petrash (Gryphon House, 2003)

- The Center on Fathers, Families, and Public Policy: Helps create a society in which low-income parents—mothers as well as fathers—are in a position to support their children emotionally, financially, and physically:
  23 N. Pinckney Street, Suite 210
  Madison, WI 53703
  608-257-3148
  www.cffpp.org

- Dads and Daughters: National advocacy non-profit for fathers and daughters:
  34 East Superior Street, Suite 200
  Duluth, MN 55802
  1-888-824-DADS
  www.dadsanddaughters.org

- Fatherhood Project: National research project that develops ways to support men's involvement in child rearing:
  fatherhoodproject.org

- National Practitioners Network for Fathers and Families: National membership organization for people and programs working to increase the responsible involvement of fathers in the lives of their children:
  www.npnff.org

- Fatherville: Where real fathers write about real fatherhood:
  www.fatherville.com

- Conscious Fathering Program: Explore, define and plan your own individual fatherhood:
  www.consciousfathering.org

- At Home Dad Network:
  www.athomedad.com

- National Compadres Network: Reinforces the positive involvement of Latino males in the lives of their children and families:
  www.nimitz.net/compadres

- National Latino Fatherhood and Family Institute: Involves Latino males involvement in their families and community:
  www.nlffi.org

- National Center for Strategic Nonprofit Planning and Community Leadership: Helps poor single fathers pull themselves out of poverty and build stronger links to their children and their children's mothers:
  2000 L Street N.W., Suite 815
  Washington, D.C. 20036
  1-888-528-NPCL, 202-822-6725
  www.npcl.org

- Center for Fathers, Families, and Workforce Development: Engages men in the fight against infant mortality and low-birth weight babies:
  www.cfwd.org

- Center for Successful Fathering: Promoting the Benefits of Involved Dads and Moms: www.fathering.org

- National Center for Fathering: Insights, information, and training to help you become a better father: www.fathers.com

- Mr. Dad: Mr. Dad (expert Armin Brott) answers questions on all aspects of fatherhood, from dads' experience during pregnancy to the social and political obstacles that hinder father involvement: www.mrdad.com

- Slowlane: Stay At Home Dads Resource: searchable collection of articles and media clips written by, for, and about primary caregiving fathers: www.Slowlane.com

- Dads Today: Dad-related resources for parents by parents: www.dadstoday.com

- The National Fatherhood Initiative: Dedicated to increasing the proportion of children growing up with involved, responsible, and committed fathers: www.fatherhood.org/

- Fathers First online: Created by author and fathering guru Pete Siler: www.fathersfirst.org

- Websites for Dads: A lot of links to sites for fathers, single dads, stay at home dads, etc.: www.earlychildhoodlinks.com/parents/ fatherhood.htm or www.fatherville.com/ fatherville-links-and-resources.shtml

- U.S. Department of Health and Human Services Fatherhood Initiative: Activities that recognize and support the roles of fathers in families: www.fatherhood.hhs.gov

- The National Center on Fathers and Families: An interdisciplinary policy research center on father involvement and family development: www.ncoff.gse.upenn.edu

Index

A

adoptions, announcing, 14-15

advice from parents, taking, 7-8

alcohol abuse, dangers of, 66

Alcoholics Anonymous (AA), 67

Alexander Technique, childbirth, 100-101

All About Sex: A Family Resource on Sex and Sexuality, 26, 31

American Academy of Husband-Coached Childbirth, 99

American College of Nurse-Midwives, 54

androgen, 27

Anka, Paul, 8

announcing
    adoptions, 14-15
    pregnancies, 10-14

Apgar tests, 155

Association of Christian Childbirth Professionals, 101

Association of Labor Assistants and Childbirth Educators, 101

B

babies, comparing to others, 119

bath water thermometers, purchasing, 91

C

W–X–Y–Z